MUHAMMAD ALI

MUHAMMAD ALI
The Fight For Respect

by
Thomas Conklin

New Directions
The Millbrook Press
Brookfield, Connecticut

Produced in association with Agincourt Press.
Interior Design: Tilman Reitzle

Photographs courtesy of: AP/Wide World Photos: cover, 16, 28, 31, 38, 49, 54, 59, 69, 83; The Bettmann Archive: 10, 52, 62, 77, 88; Steele Collection: 21; Schomburg Center for Research in Black History and Culture: 34, 73.

Library of Congress Cataloging-in-Publication Data

Conklin, Thomas.
Muhammad Ali: the fight for respect/by Thomas Conklin.

p.   cm.
"New directions."
Includes bibliographical references and index.
Summary: A biography of the colorful, controversial heavyweight champion.
ISBN 1-56294-112-7

1. Ali, Muhammad, 1942-
2. Boxers (Sports)—United States—Biography. I. Title.

GV1132.A44C66   1992
796.83'092—dc20
[B]   91–25950 CIP

To my father

Contents

Introduction   9

1   A Federal Case   11

2   A Border State   17

3   Golden Boy   29

4   The Louisville Lip   36

5   Cassius X   44

6   You'll Lose Your Money If You Bet on Sonny   53

7   Drafted   65

8   Exile and Return   71

9   Ali, Bomaye!   80

10   The Greatest   87

Important Events in Muhammad Ali's Life   95

Notes   96

Suggested Reading   98

Index   99

Introduction

I once visited Muhammad Ali's high school in Louisville, Kentucky. His teachers there remembered him with pride and affection. "He was such a nice, quiet, polite young man," one of them told me. Others agreed. They described him as a gentle, considerate, and private person.

I must admit that I was somewhat surprised by their recollections because I had come to Louisville with a quite different impression of Cassius Clay, as Ali was then known. Along with the rest of America, I had come to know the new heavyweight champion as the "Louisville Lip," a brash and talkative self-promoter. "I AM SO GREAT!" Clay had screamed after his remarkable upset of the fearsome Sonny Liston. "I . . . AM . . . THE . . . GREATEST!" People expected these outbursts because bragging was the champ's public trademark. But how could this be the same polite and private person that his teachers remembered?

Throughout his life, Muhammad Ali surprised many people. Soon after his victory over Liston, he announced that he was changing his name and converting to the Nation of Islam, a radical black religious group. Because the Nation of Islam was considered by the white American mainstream to be a group of hatemongers, all the major media attacked Ali for his conversion. But the champ paid little attention. It was the first time that he publicly followed his own path, doing only what he himself thought to be right. But it wasn't the last.

Three years later, in 1967, at the height of the Vietnam War, Ali was drafted into the army. Many people close to him begged him to join, if only to take a posting with Special Services and perform boxing exhibitions. But Ali refused, because his religious views did not permit him to serve in the army. He knew in advance that his title, and therefore his livelihood, would almost certainly be taken from him, but he never wavered in his resolve. In the end, the Supreme Court—and the nation as well—decided that he was in the right when he refused induction. But Muhammad Ali knew that all along.

Caroline Hodges Persell
Chair, Department of Sociology
New York University

Muhammad Ali with broadcaster Howard Cosell outside the U.S. Army Induction Center in Houston, Texas.

1

A Federal Case

On the morning of April 28, 1967, Muhammad Ali, the undisputed heavyweight boxing champion of the world, sat in the restaurant of the Hotel America in Houston, Texas. The newspaper that day was filled with the latest reports from Vietnam.

A mortar attack on American positions near Hue had wounded one hundred marines. In a bombing raid over Hanoi, four American planes had been shot down. Meanwhile, the eternally optimistic General William C. Westmoreland, commander of the American forces in Vietnam, was preparing to tell Congress how well the war was going. Through unrelenting military, political, and psychological pressure, he would say the next day, American forces were absolutely certain to "prevail in Vietnam over the communist aggressor."[1]

But Ali didn't pay much attention to the newspaper that day. He had other things on his mind. With him at breakfast was a trio of lawyers: Hayden Covington; Quinton Hodges; and Chauncey Eskridge, lawyer to Dr. Martin Luther King, Jr. One of them showed Ali a newspaper clipping that had been sent to him anonymously. It contained a photograph of Hodges. Across his face someone had scrawled, "Houston's great nigger lawyer."

Ali shrugged. He was used to that sort of thing by now. He and his entourage left the hotel by cab. Ali was not heading for the gym, however, to trade punches with another boxer.

His destination was the Armed Forces Examining and Entrance Station at 701 San Jacinto Street. His opponent was the government of the United States of America.

Ali's cab pulled up outside the induction center just before 8:00 A.M. A crowd of reporters, photographers, and television cameramen were waiting for him. As soon as Ali, dressed in a conservative black suit, stepped out of the cab, they surged forward, hoping for a snappy quote from the glib champion.

Ali and his attorneys made their way through the crowd without saying a word. Once inside, Ali paused a moment to gather himself, exchanged some final words with his lawyers, and entered a large room. In it were twenty-five other draftees, who stood in a silent line before a group of military officers. The officers were sitting at a table, sorting through papers.

Finally, one of the officers stood up. "First you will take a written test," he told the draftees, "then a physical examination, and then you will be called for induction. After that, you will line up outside for the bus to camp."[2]

After Ali and the others had taken the written tests, they went into another room and stripped down to their shorts, Ali revealing his near-perfect champion's physique. When the physical examination was over, the draftees were served box lunches. Inside each were beef and ham sandwiches, an apple, an orange, and a piece of cake. Although Ali was hungry, he threw away the ham sandwich. His Muslim religion did not allow him to eat pork.

After lunch, the draftees were led into Room 1B, where they stood before a young army officer, Lt. S. Steven Dunkley. "Attention!" Dunkley shouted. The draftees straightened up. "You are about to be inducted into the Armed Forces of the

United States....You will take one step forward as your name and service are called, and such step will constitute your induction...."

Dunkley looked down at the roster and began to call names: "Jason Adams—Army; John Allen—Navy; Leroy Bradlow—Army; Luis Cerrato—Army..." As each name was called, the draftee stepped forward. Then Dunkley paused. He cleared his throat and called out in a loud voice: "Cassius Clay—Army!"

Muhammad Ali, born Cassius Clay twenty-five years earlier, didn't move. Dunkley looked up and stared Ali in the eye. "Cassius Clay! Will you please step forward and be inducted into the Armed Forces of the United States?"

Ali stood perfectly still. He knew there would be consequences—most likely criminal charges and the possibility of five years in prison. Almost certainly he would lose the heavyweight title and be banned from the ring.

"Cassius Clay—Army!" cried Dunkley.

When Ali still refused to move, Lt. Clarence Hartman stepped forward and handed him a form. "Would you please sign this statement and give your reasons for refusing induction?"[3] Ali did so.

At 1:10 P.M., Lieutenant Colonel J. Edwin McKee of the Houston police force led Ali to a makeshift press room filled with reporters. McKee read a prepared statement announcing that Cassius Clay, also known as Muhammad Ali, had refused induction into the United States armed services. Then he introduced Ali.

The reporters barked their questions, but the usually talkative Ali didn't say a word. He simply handed out copies of his own prepared statement and left the room with his lawyers. Ali's statement read in part:

It is in the light of my consciousness as a Muslim minister and my personal convictions that I take my stand in rejecting the call to be admitted in the armed services. I do so with the full realization of its implications and possible consequences. I have searched my conscience and I find I cannot be true to my belief in my religion by accepting such a call.…

I strongly object to the fact that so many newspapers have given the American public and the world the impression that I have only two alternatives in taking this stand: either I go to jail or I go to the Army. There is another alternative, and that alternative is justice.[4]

One hour later, Ali was stripped of his title and banned from the ring. Ten days later, he was formally charged with the crime of draft evasion. Once Ali was indicted for draft evasion, his passport was revoked. For the next three years, the heavyweight boxing champion of the world would live in what amounted to internal exile.

In April, 1967, Muhammad Ali was arguably the most famous man in the world, but some critics would have said that "notorious" described him more accurately. It had been twenty years since Jackie Robinson and Joe Louis had set the standard of behavior for the star black athlete. Off the field and outside the ring, Robinson and Louis were quiet, humble, deferential men. "They're a credit to their race" was a common compliment.

But Muhammad Ali was different, free-spirited. He spoke his mind and boasted. He publicly taunted his opponents. Ali refused to be a humble "white man's negro." He was also one of the finest boxers who ever fought.

Ali first burst into the national consciousness during the 1960 Olympics when, as eighteen-year-old Cassius Clay of Louisville, Kentucky, he loudly proclaimed, "I'm the Greatest!" and backed up his words with a gold medal. Four years later, he was the heavyweight champion of the world. People liked the brash, funny, charismatic young fighter. But when he announced his conversion to an extremist black religion, the Nation of Islam, attitudes toward him changed.

That April day in 1967, however, when Muhammad Ali refused to take part in a war he considered wrong, he took a greater step than any black American athlete or celebrity had taken before. Some blacks had been accepted into white society; others had courageously confronted the white power structure, demanding dignity and equality and often paying for their dreams with their lives. But Ali was one of the first successful blacks outside of politics to use his position to defy convention and stand up for his beliefs. And by doing so, he risked losing everything.

Cassius Clay at age 12.

2

A Border State

It was a rainy day in October of 1954. Oil that had leaked from the passing traffic made rainbows on the black asphalt streets of downtown Louisville, Kentucky. Two twelve-year-old boys rode their bicycles through the drizzle, but as the rain grew harder, the two friends decided to make for the Columbia Auditorium, where the annual Louisville Home Show was being held. Word had it that free popcorn and hot dogs were available at the show.

The boys spent the rest of the afternoon eating. It wasn't until seven o'clock that they finally staggered out into the rain, only to find that one of their bikes—a shiny red Schwinn, with chrome trim and a spotlight—had been stolen.

Angry and frightened, the boys looked all over for the bike, with no luck. Then a passerby suggested they report the theft to the nearest policeman, a traffic cop named Joe Martin, who ran a boxing gym in the basement of the convention hall. As the two boys ran down the stairs to the gym, Cassius Clay, the one whose bike had been stolen, blinked back tears of rage and frustration.

"There were about ten boxers in the gym," he would later recall, "some hitting the speed bag, some in the ring, sparring, some jumping rope. I stood there, smelling the sweat and rubbing alcohol, and a feeling of awe come over me.... The sights and sounds and smell of the boxing gym excited me so much that I almost forgot about the bike."[1] Young Cassius Clay had discovered boxing.

Cassius Marcellus Clay, Jr., was born in Louisville on January 17, 1942. He was named after his father, who had in turn been named after the white 19th century political leader Cassius Marcellus Clay.

The original Cassius Marcellus Clay had been a friend to Lincoln, the United States ambassador to Russia in the 1860s, and an ardent abolitionist. He freed his own slaves long before the Thirteenth Amendment abolished all slavery; and on more than one occasion, he fired his rifle at neighbors in defense of his views. Cassius Marcellus Clay, Jr., was himself a direct descendant of the slaves freed by the original Cassius Marcellus Clay almost a century earlier.

Both Clays grew up in a town and a state torn by contradictions. Kentucky was called a "border state" during the Civil War because it remained neutral. To call it a "divided state" would have been more accurate, however. The leaders of the Union and the Confederacy—Abraham Lincoln and Jefferson Davis—were both natives of Kentucky. And although Kentucky never seceded from the Union, neither did it abolish slavery on its own. It took the Thirteenth Amendment to end slavery in Kentucky.

By the middle of the twentieth century, Louisville, the largest city in Kentucky, was still a place of profound contradictions. On the one hand, it was the seat of fabulous wealth. Among the people who made their home in Louisville were the Reynolds family, makers of Reynolds Wrap and other kitchen products; the proprietors of Brown-Forman, one of the country's largest distilleries; and many of the wealthiest tobacco growers in the South. Louisville was also home to the famous Churchill Downs racetrack, named after the beautiful, gently rolling hills on whose pastures the finest thoroughbred horses in the United States were raised.

Amid this great wealth, however, downtown Louisville remained the site of devastating poverty. The worst neighborhood was a dead-end black ghetto, known to locals as "Snake Town."

Along with the rest of the South during the 1940s and 1950s, Louisville was burdened with the most divisive issue of the century: the segregation of blacks and whites. Segregation was supposed to keep the races "separate but equal." But in reality, segregation stripped away the rights of many blacks, as well as much of their sense of human dignity. Restaurants, bathrooms, drinking fountains, and even phone booths were designated "white only." The Atlanta zoo refused to allow blacks and whites to visit on the same day. Separate Bibles were used to swear oaths in court. Blacks had their own—generally shabbier—hotels, restaurants, and taverns. They were also forced to ride at the back of public buses and to sit in separate train compartments.

Although young Cassius Clay didn't grow up in Snake Town, he and his family lived under these segregated conditions in a black working-class section of town. His father, Cassius Marcellus Clay, Sr., known as Cash, had been an aspiring artist in his youth. Cassius, Jr.'s mother, Odessa, was a pretty, vivacious woman. Together, they would have one other child, a second son named Rudy.

Cassius, Jr., was a boisterous baby, who demonstrated his pugilistic skills at an extremely young age. "I was spanking him and he got mad and swung at me," his mother remembered. "[He] knocked both of my two front teeth out of place. He was only a year old then. It shows how hard he could hit from the start."[2]

The Clays were part of a large, tightly knit family. The patriarch was Cassius, Jr.'s grandfather, the muscular, handsome Herman Clay. Herman's first job had been cleaning spittoons in Louisville's "white only" taverns for twenty-five cents a week. Through hard-work and determination, he managed to start his own business, selling ice and wood back in the days before blacks in Louisville could afford electric refrigerators and oil furnaces. Once he became a successful businessman, though, Herman Clay refused to allow white men to enter his home, remembering how they had treated him while he cleaned their barroom floors.

Herman's son, Cash, had dreamed as a young man of leaving the South to fulfill his potential as an artist. "Go to New York, Chicago, somewhere," his family advised him. "The South [is] no place for a colored artist."[3] But Cash had to balance his artistic ambitions against his responsibilities as a husband and father, so he became a professional sign painter. A few years after Cassius, Jr., was born, Cash bought a house for his family on Louisville's Grand Avenue for $4,500. Though the street may have been called Grand, the house was less so. It was small, with bad plumbing and a leaky roof.

Still, for a southern black of the time, Cash Clay was doing quite well. He owned a house and didn't have to work at an assembly-line job or in the cotton fields. But the monthly mortgage payments were enough to force him to abandon his artistic ambitions. So he painted signs full time, while his wife cleaned the homes of white families at a daily wage of four dollars. Nonetheless, by the standards of the day, the Clays were solidly in the black middle class.

Like his father and grandfather before him, Cassius, Jr., grew up to be handsome and articulate. And like most kids, he was apt to get into trouble. "He should have been a baseball player," his mother said. "He was always throwing rocks in the street."[4]

It was his father's wish that Cassius study hard to become a teacher or a lawyer, but the boy was never a gifted student. In school, he studied mechanical drawing and drafting. After school, he helped out his father on large jobs, running up and down the ladder with paint.

Though hatred of segregation burned less hotly in him than in others of his generation, young Cassius was nonetheless aware of the racial injustice all around him. One incident in particular made a huge impression. "When I was growing up, a colored boy named Emmett Till was murdered in Mississippi for whistling at a white woman," he later recalled. "Emmett Till was the same age as me, and even though they caught the men who did it, nothing happened to them. Things like that went on all the time."[5]

Emmett Till

During the summer of 1955, fourteen-year-old Emmett Till had traveled from his home in Chicago to visit some relatives in Money, Mississippi. One day, on a dare, Till went into the town's general store, bought some candy, and on his way out said, "Bye, baby" to the white girl behind the counter. Not a native to the Deep South, Till didn't understand the significance of what he had done.

Three days later, at two-thirty in the morning, two white men with guns came to the house where Till was staying and demanded the boy. A week later, his body was found at the bottom of the Tallahatchie River with a seventy-pound cotton-gin fan tied to his neck with barbed wire. The two men were tried for the crime, but despite eyewitness testimony, they were found to be innocent. In his summation, one defense lawyer told the all-white jury that he was sure "every last Anglo-Saxon one of you has the courage to free these men."[6]

In Louisville, there were other dangers facing Cassius during his teen years, such as the lure of Snake Town's mean streets and the temptation to join a gang. Perhaps his parents were thinking of these things when Cassius came home that rainy day without his bike, but with an application from Joe Martin's boxing gym instead. In any case, they allowed him to join.

At that time, boxing was one of the few fields in which a talented young black man could hope to succeed on a grand scale. Segregation was still the law in southern universities, and as a result much in the way of professional achievement was closed to blacks. In the sports world, baseball and football had only recently been integrated. Boxing, however, already had a long tradition of black success dating back to Jack Johnson, the first black heavyweight champion, who won the title in 1908. Later, during the late 1930s and early

1940s, heavyweight champ Joe Louis championed the cause of racial justice, especially in his fights with the pride of the racist Nazis, the German fighter Max Schmeling.

It was important for a young fighter to find the right place to develop his skills. Fortunately, Joe Martin's gym was the perfect place for Cassius Clay. He learned how to fight there, and he also learned how to promote himself. Martin produced a local television show called "Tomorrow's Champions," which featured young boxers from his gym in three-round bouts. Boys who fought on the show earned four dollars for each appearance, as well as a chance to become local celebrities. Six weeks after he joined the gym, and weighing only eighty-nine pounds, Cassius Marcellus Clay, Jr., was picked by Martin to fight on the show.

It was a dream come true for Cassius, and it foreshadowed much of his later career. He spent the week before the fight hard at work, hyping it. He went around Louisville, knocking on doors and telling complete strangers, "I'm Cassius Clay, and I'm having a fight on television. I hope you'll watch me."[7] Then he'd tell them the date, time, and channel of the broadcast.

The brash young Clay won his first fight in a split decision over the now immortalized Ronnie O'Keefe. His father was thrilled. Watching on television as the decision was announced, Cash yelled that his boy was going to be the next world heavyweight champion. When Cassius arrived home, his father told him, "Let's get ready for it. Get down to business. I've got another Joe Louis!"[8]

Cash may have seen his son as the second coming of Louis, but young Cassius decided that he'd rather emulate Sugar Ray Robinson, the perennially popular middleweight champion. Sugar Ray was known as much for his speed and guile inside the ring as for his flamboyant personality outside it. Because of his great and uncompromising success, Robinson served as both an inspiration and an important role model to the young, impressionable Clay.

For the next three years, Cassius worked hard on his boxing. He had always been quick, but soon he developed some technique to match his cunning. And in 1957, he took another giant step in his self-promotion. Light-heavyweight contender Willie Pastrano was in Louisville for a fight. Pastrano was hanging out in his hotel room, watching television with his trainer, Angelo Dundee, when the phone rang. Dundee answered.

"This is Cassius Clay, the next heavyweight champion talking," bragged the voice on the phone. "I'm gonna win the Olympics and be heavyweight champ. I'm in the lobby. Can I come up?"[9]

Dundee turned to Pastrano. "Some kind of nut is on the phone telling me all his attributes, and he wants to come up. What do you say?"

"OK, man," said Pastrano. "I'm tired of this TV. Invite him up, and maybe we'll get some kicks."[10]

When Dundee opened the door a few minutes later, the "nut" turned out to be a tall, skinny, fifteen-year-old kid. But he walked into the room as though he owned the place, and after introducing himself again, Clay spent the next few hours with the old pros, pumping them for tips and boxing lore. When he finally left, Cassius Clay reassured Pastrano and Dundee that he would, indeed, be the heavyweight champion one day.

"Can you believe that?" Dundee asked years later, shaking his head at the audacity of the young Clay. "Can you believe he was fifteen years old at the time?"[11]

But there was no doubt in Cassius's mind that he had what it took. He got up every morning and ran up to six miles in the park before school. Then he fit in another, shorter run during lunch. After school, he worked for four hours doing odd jobs at Nazareth College, before crossing the street for a two-hour workout at Joe Martin's gym. Some nights and weekends, he rode his motor scooter all the way across town for late-night sessions with a black trainer named Fred Stoner.

"It's safe to say," remembers Martin, "that Cassius believed in himself right from the beginning.... It was impossible to discourage him. He was easily the hardest worker of any kid I ever taught, and I've taught hundreds in my time."[12]

Cassius had more going for him than just heart, though. He was tall, lanky, and—most importantly—fast. As time went on, he developed a unique style to take advantage of his strengths. While most boxers learn to cover up and absorb punches with their gloves, Cassius developed what he called "built-in radar," the uncanny ability to "slip" punches by moving his head. "I learn[ed] to put my head within hitting range, force my opponent to throw blows, then lean back and away, keeping [my] eyes wide open, so I [could] see everything," he explained. "It takes a lot out of a fighter to throw punches that land in thin air."[13]

Clay was also developing an incredible physique. By the time he was 18 years old, Cassius stood six feet, two inches tall and weighed 178 pounds of muscle. And he still wasn't finished growing.

Clay set a grueling schedule for himself. In order to earn a shot at the professional heavyweight championship, he would first have to prove himself as an amateur. Between 1954 and 1960, he fought 108 amateur bouts, winning all but eight of them. His titles included the National Golden Gloves heavyweight and Amateur Athletic Union light-heavyweight championships, both of which he won two years in a row.

His intensive training schedule left little time for studying, but his teachers understood that Cassius Clay's best chance for greatness lay in the ring, not in the classroom. "We planned his program to help him in his career," his high school principal, Atwood Wilson, said. "He took courses like income tax and accounting. We didn't want him to make financial mistakes like some other fighters [had]."[14]

A few years after Clay showed up at their hotel room, Pastrano and Dundee returned to Louisville for another fight. This time, Pastrano met Cassius in a different setting. Clay had been hired as one of Pastrano's sparring partners.

The first time they climbed into the ring together, Pastrano looked slow and stale. None of his punches were landing. He looked old. Dundee stopped the session after one round and took his fighter aside. "You looked terrible, man" he told Pastrano. "What's the matter with you?" Pastrano shook his head and nodded at Clay. "This cat is a good one, Angie," he said.[15]

Cassius Clay was on the verge of greatness. His next step was clear: to make the 1960 Olympic team and win gold in Rome. After that, he could position himself for his ultimate goal, the world heavyweight championship.

One major obstacle that stood in his way, however, was a lack of money. An amateur boxer needed a lot of financial support to pay for his training expenses, because it was impossible to train seriously while at the same time holding down a regular job. Fortunately, some of the local Louisville aristocracy had noticed Clay's success and taken an interest in him. One of these people, Billy Reynolds, heir to the Reynolds aluminum foil fortune, became a patron of sorts to the ambitious young boxer. After high school, Reynolds offered Clay a job that wouldn't require much effort and would therefore allow the fighter time to train.

As Clay rode out to the Reynolds estate for his first day of work, he wondered what sort of job he'd be doing. He hoped it might help him develop the mechanical drawing skills he'd acquired in school, and thus prepare him for a career beyond the ring. When he got to the mansion, however, Clay discovered that he was to be Billy Reynolds's "houseboy," cleaning the stables and scrubbing the toilets.

Clay didn't complain. Instead, with the money he made he bought the first decent boxing equipment he'd owned in his life. And there was another benefit to the job. In addition to paying him a good salary, Billy Reynolds had his cook feed Clay an excellent lunch every day. He ate it on the back porch, alongside Reynolds's prize dogs.

"I didn't really mind then," he remembered years later. "I made friends with some excellent breeds of dogs."[16]

Clay in training for the 1960 Olympics in Rome.

3

Golden Boy

"With matchless aplomb these noblest of Romans bridged the centuries and produced a set of Olympic Games in 1960 that would have dwarfed into insignificance the most elaborate spectacles of Nero or Caligula or any other of the ancient emperors...."[1]

So wrote a *New York Times* sports reporter describing the 1960 Rome Olympics. And the Games were dazzling that year, more spectacular even than the *Times* reporter's prose. For the first time since World War II, money was no object. The Italian government had financed the Games through a successful weekly lottery on professional soccer that had raised $30 million. That was quite a princely sum in 1960, and the Italian Organizing Committee was determined to get its money's worth.

Many of the ancient Olympic events, such as gymnastics and wrestling, were held in historic Roman ruins. The modern events, such as boxing and basketball, were slated for the newly constructed Palazzo della Sport. There was also a new swimming facility and a magnificent Olympic Village, complete with shopping centers and parks, to host the athletes.

Even more impressive than the Olympic Village, though, was the talent it housed: a record 5,902 competitors from eighty-four nations, certainly the finest collection of Olympic athletes the world had yet seen. In the twenty-five men's track and field events, for example, twenty-one Olympic records were broken. Among the stars of the American team were decathlete Rafer Johnson, known as "the World's Greatest Athlete," and Wilma Rudolph, who tied the world record in the women's 100-meter dash. It was eighteen-year-old Cassius Clay of Louisville, Kentucky, however, who made the biggest splash.

Clay was in Rome that summer to fight for the lightheavyweight gold. He had earned a spot on the Olympic boxing team by winning the Olympic trials in San Francisco. "He's a better prospect…than Floyd Patterson was," reported one Olympic boxing official. "[Clay] has the quickest hands I've ever seen for a light heavyweight."[2] Patterson, the world heavyweight champion in 1960, had won an Olympic gold medal himself in 1954.

Never one to be shy, Clay lived it up in Rome. He was always on the move, always talking to new and different people from all over the world. As one reporter wrote, he "seemed to be running for mayor of the Olympic Village."[3] Clay spent so much time meeting and joking with his fellow athletes that his coach worried he might be too tired to fight.

Clay certainly found enough ways to distract himself, but he still managed to stay focused on his goal: the Olympic gold. Clay's first match in the single-elimination tournament was against Belgium's Yvon Becus, whom he easily defeated. In the next round, he faced a Russian, Gennady Shatkov, who staggered Clay with a shot to the head. "I didn't even know where I was at," Clay admitted later.[4] But he pulled himself together and came back to win a unanimous decision.

In the semifinals, Clay outpointed Argentina's Tony Madigan, a dangerous fighter who had beaten him the previous year in one of Clay's few amateur defeats. Now all that stood between Cassius Clay and the gold medal was the European champion, Poland's Zbigniew Pietrzykowski, a tall, blond southpaw. "Pietrzykowski was virtually unbeatable in Europe," wrote a veteran British boxing reporter. "And yet Clay boxed rings around him, cutting his face to pieces in the process."[5]

If he had seemed cheerful before, winning the gold made Clay delirious. For the next forty-eight hours, he refused to remove the medal from around his neck. "First time in my life I ever slept on my back," he told a reporter. "Had to, or that medal would have cut my chest."[6]

Upon his return from Rome, Clay was treated by Billy Reynolds to a stay in New York City. Still wearing his Olympic blazer and gold medal, Clay stopped traffic in Times Square as jaded cabbies called out their congratulations on his Olympic success. Strangers jumped at the opportunity to shake the champ's hand. He had come a long way from Billy Reynolds's back porch.

An Italian fan admires Clay's gold medal.

While in town, Clay stayed at Reynolds's apartment at the Waldorf Astoria, then one of New York's swankest addresses. Reynolds's suite was next door to that of a former king of England and three floors down from the apartment of former President Herbert Hoover. Clay ate it up. "Man, this is the life," he told one of the many reporters trailing him.[7]

Having reached the pinnacle of amateur success, Clay now had a decision to make. It was time for him to consider turning pro, normally a delicate judgment, but the high life he tasted in New York made the choice easy for him. "I'm the amateur light-heavyweight champ of the world, and I don't have a penny," Clay announced. "Just as soon as I get the right people to handle me, I'm turning pro."[8]

Cassius Clay's decision to become a professional boxer was big news on the sports pages, but there was bigger news on the front pages that fall of 1960. On October 19, a month after Clay's visit to New York City, Dr. Martin Luther King, Jr., was sentenced to four month's hard labor in a Georgia prison. He had been charged with technical violations of an earlier probation involving a traffic violation. But the sentence was actually a reprisal for his activities as a civil rights leader.

Six years earlier, in 1954, the twenty-five-year-old King had moved to Montgomery, Alabama, to take over as minister of the Dexter Avenue Baptist Church. His first year there was relatively uneventful, but then something unexpected happened. On December 1, 1955, Rosa Parks refused to give up her seat on a city bus, as local segregation laws required, so that a white passenger could sit down. After the arrest of Mrs. Parks, King and his fellow black ministers organized a boycott of the city buses that lasted for more than a year. By the time it ended, the Montgomery Bus Boycott had made national headlines and elevated King to a prominent leadership role in the increasingly confrontational fight for black civil rights.

In 1954, the year King moved to Montgomery, the Supreme Court had ruled in the landmark case *Brown v. Board of Education* that the "separate but equal" standard behind the segregation laws of the South was unconstitutional, at least when it was applied to public education. State and local governments in Mississippi, Alabama, and elsewhere, however, refused to obey the court's ruling and maintained two separate public school systems, one for whites and one for blacks. In 1957, President Dwight Eisenhower had to send federal troops into Little Rock, Arkansas, to enforce a court order integrating Central High School there.

During the late 1950s, it became clear to King and others that winning in the courts would not be enough in itself to end segregation. Southern states were simply ignoring the court decisions and continuing to enforce segregation. Black leaders realized that they would have to take more direct action.

Exactly one month into the new decade, on February 1, 1960, four black freshmen from the North Carolina Agricultural and Technical College sat down at a Woolworth's lunch counter in downtown Greensboro. The lunch counter was for whites only, but the young men ordered coffee anyway. The waitress behind the counter refused to serve them and told them to leave. But the four college students refused to leave, saying they wouldn't get up until they were served.

Finally, the store closed, and the four young men— Franklin McCain, Joseph McNeil, David Richmond, and Ezell Blair, Jr.—returned to campus, where they were amazed by what they found. Within the space of a single afternoon, they had become heroes. On their return from the lunch counter, their fellow students cheered them for the courage they had displayed in confronting segregation head-on.

The next day, the lunch counter of the Greensboro Woolworth's was clogged with twenty black students from North Carolina A&T, all of whom refused to leave until they were served. Soon, white students from a nearby women's college joined the demonstration, and within a few weeks the protests spread to other lunch counters in other cities. In these sit-ins, the civil rights movement found a new and potent weapon, and by the summer, they were everywhere—shopping centers, drugstores, and theaters all over the South.

In the wake of the sit-ins, civil rights became a singularly controversial and divisive issue. It even touched the Rome Olympics that fall. Looking to embarrass the United States,

This whites-only lunch counter closed rather than serve black customers.

Soviet journalists often prodded young black athletes from the South to condemn the segregation they experienced at home. One Soviet reporter even approached America's light-heavyweight gold medalist.

"You tell your readers we got qualified people working on that, and I'm not worried about the outcome," Cassius Clay said. "To me, the U.S.A. is still the best country in the world.... It may be hard to get something to eat sometimes, but anyhow [I'm not] fighting alligators and living in a mud hut."[9] Clay would later come to regret those words.

After his tour of New York City, Clay returned to a hero's welcome in Louisville. The mayor presented him with the key to the city, and the governor slapped him on the back. When Clay finally made it back to Grand Avenue, he saw that his father had painted the front steps of their house red, white, and blue. News photographers snapped pictures of Cassius and his father, standing on their front porch, singing the national anthem.

Clay's experiences in Rome and New York, however, began to influence his thinking about his identity as a black American. In Rome, he had been accepted as one of an elite group of athletes. In New York, he had been hailed as a conquering hero. Yet in Louisville, he was still Cassius Clay—a local colored boy who had made good, but still a colored boy.

One day not long after his return from Rome, Clay dropped by a Louisville luncheonette for a hamburger. He was refused service. Clay politely pointed out that he was no ordinary customer, that he was Louisville's famous gold-medal winner. The waitress was impressed. She ran to tell her boss that Cassius Clay wanted service.

"I don't give a damn who he is," the owner roared. "I told you. We don't serve niggers!"[10]

4

The Louisville Lip

Cassius Clay made his professional boxing debut against Tunney Hunsaker on October 29, 1960. He and his father handled the arrangements. Hunsaker was an obscure but experienced boxer, as well as the police chief of a small West Virginia town.

In addition to serving as his own promoter, Clay also trained himself, a decision that almost cost him the fight. Shortly before stepping into the ring, he ate two steaks, then came close to losing them when Hunsaker connected with a punch to the stomach. This proved to be the only moment Clay was in trouble, however, and he won a unanimous six-round decision. Nonetheless, it was clear even before the Hunsaker fight that Clay needed truly professional guidance if he were to develop sufficiently to break into the big-money fight game. He had earlier asked two of his heroes, Joe Louis and Sugar Ray Robinson, if they would train him, but both had declined.

There were other takers, however, because Cassius Clay, Olympic gold medalist, was a hot property. Among those angling to become Clay's manager were his pre-Olympic patron Billy Reynolds, former Olympic heavyweight champion Pete Rademacher, and Cus D'Amato—the manager of Floyd Patterson and, much later, Mike Tyson.

The Clays considered each offer carefully. Finally, Cash Clay advised his son to turn them all down so that Cassius, Jr., could retain as much control over his own career as possible.

Three days before the Hunsaker fight, Cassius came to terms with a group of local businessmen who called themselves the Louisville Sponsoring Group. Their sole property was Cassius Marcellus Clay.

The money they offered Clay was astronomical for the time: a cash signing bonus of $10,000, training expenses for the next six years, and a monthly salary of $333. In exchange, they would receive 50 percent of Clay's earnings for the first four years of the contract and 40 percent during the remaining two years.

When Elvis Presley got his first large check from a record company, he went right out and bought his mother a brand-new pink Cadillac. That's also what Clay did with his first bonus money, although the Cadillac Clay bought wasn't pink. The balance of the $10,000 he used to repair his parents' house and pay off the mortgage.

Now that his financial situation was taken care of, Clay's next order of business was to find a suitable trainer. At first, he turned to another black boxing legend, the one-time light-heavyweight champ Archie Moore.

Clay arrived at Moore's San Diego camp eager to begin his assault on the heavyweight title. But Moore preached patience and imposed on Clay a strict training regimen—lots of sparring, roadwork, drilling in the basics, and little else. It wasn't what Clay had in mind, not what he had in mind at all. After just a few weeks, he left.

From San Diego, Clay headed for Miami and Angelo Dundee. Dundee had a "hands-off" training method in sharp contrast to Archie Moore's belief that all boxers should fight Archie Moore's way. Dundee allowed each fighter to establish his own style and then tried to develop that style to its fullest potential.

Clay with his trainer, Angelo Dundee.

Clay and Dundee turned out to be perfectly suited for one another, and they forged a working relationship that lasted twenty years. "I never talked to him while he was working in the gym or while he was fighting," Dundee explained. "I don't think you can help a fighter much that way, because by the time he has listened to you and tried to understand what you're saying and then tried to do what you said to do, it's too late."[1]

Dundee and the Louisville Sponsoring Group decided to bring Clay along slowly, which is boxing shorthand for having a young fighter face a few has-beens and never-weres to get his feet wet. Clay realized the importance of this strategy, but it bored him. It wasn't until June 26, 1961, in Las Vegas that Clay took on the fighter Dundee later claimed was his first real professional challenge—a tall, awkward boxer named Duke Sabedong.

The match was an important learning experience for Clay because it forced him to think in the ring. Because of his height and build, Sabedong was a gawky puncher unlike any Clay had faced before. It took a series of adjustments before Clay figured out how to pummel him.

More importantly, though, Clay discovered in Las Vegas an outlet for his ego and his sense of humor. "Up until then …he wasn't a particularly boasting man," Dundee remembered. "But while we were in Vegas he was on a sports program on the radio with Gorgeous George, the wrestler.

"Cassius just said the usual things about how he expected a tough fight and Sabedong was good, and so on," continued Dundee. "Then the announcer started talking to Gorgeous George, and George told him how he was going to tear up his opponent and they shouldn't even allow the match because he was so much better…. Clay got a big kick out of it."[2]

Clay picked up on George's technique immediately, and soon sportswriters were competing to come up with the best nickname for the loud young fighter. "Gaseous Cassius" and "The Louisville Lip" were just two of many. Within a short time, Clay became as famous for his boastful antics and outrageous self-confidence as he was for his skills in the ring.

The moment he was upstaged by Gorgeous George, Clay saw the great promotional potential of such a public attitude. Then Clay went beyond George. Not content merely to brag, Clay started praising himself in verse:

This is the story about a man
With iron fists and a beautiful tan.
He talks a lot and boasts indeed
Of a power punch and blinding speed.[3]

Next Clay began to predict the round in which he would knock out each of his unworthy opponents. One of Clay's most important early bouts came in November of 1962, against his one-time trainer, Archie Moore. Before the fight, Clay boasted:

Archie's been living off the fat of the land—
I'm here to give him his pension plan.
When you come to the fight don't block the door,
'Cause you'll all go home after Round Four.[4]

Sure enough, Clay knocked out Moore in the fourth round. The victory over a former champ was newsworthy in and of itself, but the fact that Clay had so decisively and accurately predicted the outcome made the story truly special. Sportswriters couldn't get enough of the astonishingly quotable Clay, and the media extravaganza that followed the Moore fight, more than any other single factor, made Clay immediately one of the top contenders for the heavyweight crown.

The Moore fight marked the beginning of a remarkable, and mutually beneficial, association between Clay and the sports press, which from the first had mixed feelings about the supremely confident young fighter. Star athletes at that time were a lot more humble than Clay, and mutual respect between competitors was universally considered the key to good sportsmanship. Clay's outrageous braggadocio flew in the face of the image of the modest black superstar cultivated by Joe Louis and Jackie Robinson, among others. Many sports-writers resented it. If only Clay's poems proclaiming his own beauty and strength didn't make such great copy! As the cel-ebrated boxing correspondent A.J. Liebling wrote, "There was a limitless demand for his verse, which saved sports-writers who interviewed him from having to think up gags of their own."[5]

In fact, a star of Clay's charisma and potential magnitude was just what the sport of boxing needed. There hadn't been a fighter as interesting, as provocative, as Clay in quite some time, perhaps not since the widely reviled Jack Johnson, the first black heavyweight champion. Johnson, too, was boister-ous, with lightning reflexes and a rich sense of humor. As champion from 1908 until 1915, he became famous for his love of the high life, his gold teeth, and his taunting of opponents.

White fight fans of the time hated Johnson with a passion that most people today would find difficult to believe. They ached for his defeat and desperately yearned for a "Great White Hope" to put the flamboyant champ in his place. Even former champion Jim Jeffries, then 35 years old, was dragged out of retirement to face Johnson. "Jim Jeffries must now emerge from his alfalfa farm and remove that golden smile from John-son's face," wrote the prominent author and journalist Jack London. "Jeff, it's up to you. The White Man must be res-cued."[6] Johnson whipped Jeffries in fifteen brutal rounds.

After Johnson was finally beaten by Jess Willard in 1915, twenty-two years would pass before the organizations that controlled boxing allowed another black man to fight for the heavyweight crown. That fighter was Joe Louis, a quiet, sub-dued sharecropper's son from Alabama, by way of Detroit. It was Louis's first trainer, Jack Blackburn, who gave him the advice that did more perhaps than even his boxing talent to earn him a shot at the title. "When you beat a white man," Blackburn told Louis, "never, don't ever, smile!"[7]

By nature a shy, demure man, Joe Louis set the standard of behavior for successful black athletes for many years to come. He never boasted, was always polite, and always expressed respect for his white opponents. For black Americans, however, Louis represented far more than a skilled athlete. He was a symbol of dignity and respect. Many blacks, though, were afraid to express their feelings for him. Once, when civil rights leader Jesse Jackson was a child in South Carolina, he and a friend stood outside a cigar store, listening to Louis fight a white contender. "Joe Louis was battering the guy without mercy," Jackson remembered. "But we didn't dare show any emotion over a black man beating a white one. We knew it would anger the white shopkeeper and his friends."[8]

Louis was a true champion. His titanic bouts with Max Schmeling helped make boxing one of the most popular spectator sports in the country. But after he retired, when it became clear that there was no one of Louis's stature to succeed him, the popularity of boxing took a nosedive.

Meanwhile, a shady organization known as the International Boxing Club (IBC) had surreptitiously taken control of professional boxing. Rumors spread quickly of fixed fights and mob coercion. Soon the IBC, which promoted fights on television and determined match-ups around the country, came to be known as "Octopus Inc." because of its stranglehold on the sport. By the mid-1950s, you couldn't hold a title fight in this country without the sanction of the allegedly crooked IBC.

Then, in 1956, white champion Rocky Marciano retired and the heavyweight title came up for grabs. On November

30, 1956, in Chicago, it was won by ex-Olympian Floyd Patterson, a proud young black man who refused to let the IBC pick his opponents. A few years later, the Supreme Court put the IBC out of business permanently for violating federal antitrust laws, which prohibit monopolistic practices.

During Patterson's reign, a new era of big money fights was just getting underway. The IBC had made its money promoting fights on free television, but a new system had recently been devised that would allow people in movie theaters and auditoriums around the country, or around the world, to see a fight as it happened. The system was called closed-circuit television because it allowed promoters to control the signal. Only those who paid for a ticket would see the fight. This meant that a prize fight's "gate"—the money paid by spectators—could increase beyond the capacity of a single arena, or the IBC's wildest dreams. The time was right for a young, skilled, telegenic fighter to recapture the imagination of the American public.

5

Cassius X

Sonny Liston was feeling pretty satisfied with himself. He had just destroyed heavyweight champ Floyd Patterson, knocking him out in the first round of their September, 1962, title fight. And now, as Liston trained in Las Vegas for a rematch with Patterson, sportswriters were hailing him as the meanest, toughest, most invulnerable boxer of all time. "The King Kong of boxing," one columnist wrote. "The ultimate weapon in unarmed combat, a human destroyer...."[1]

Liston decided to give himself a break a few nights before the July, 1963, rematch. He wanted to take advantage of Las Vegas's attractions, specifically its gambling.

People recognized Liston as soon as he walked into the casino of the Thunderbird Hotel. He was an enormous, bear-like man. Though only six-foot one, Liston weighed 214 pounds and was built like a tree trunk. His fists were fifteen inches in circumference, the largest of any heavyweight champion ever. His reach was eighty-four inches, longer than any except that of the six-foot, six-inch Primo Carnera, who held the title briefly in the 1930s.

Las Vegas was a long way from the dirt-poor sharecropper's farm where Liston had been raised along with his twenty-two brothers and sisters. He was often in trouble as a young man, and eventually he was convicted of armed robbery and sent to prison. There, a concerned chaplain convinced Liston to take up boxing as a means of releasing his anger and aggression.

The combination of huge fists, tremendous strength, and an endless reach made Liston practically untouchable in the ring. And Liston's attitude helped him as well. He was a sullen, brooding man, whose only real pleasure in life seemed to be knocking out other fighters. In the first year of a professional career that began in 1954 with his release from prison, Liston lost a split decision to a fighter named Marty Marshall. Seven months later, he knocked Marshall out in a rematch. Liston kept knocking people out until Floyd Patterson agreed to fight him. Then he knocked out Patterson.

"Sonny Liston had everybody scared stiff," boxing publicist Harold Conrad recalled. "People talk about [Mike] Tyson before he got beat, but Liston, when he was champ, was more ferocious, more indestructible, and everyone thought, unbeatable. This was a guy who got arrested a hundred times, went to prison for armed robbery, got out, went back again for beating up a cop, and wound up being managed by organized crime.

"When Sonny gave you the evil eye," Conrad continued, "I don't care who you were—you shrunk to two feet tall. And one thing more: He could fight like hell. They forget it now, but when Liston was champ, some people thought he was the greatest heavyweight of all time."[2]

Liston walked up to the craps table and placed a bet. The croupier handed him the dice. Liston began to lose, badly. The tension around the table grew as the crowd that had gathered to watch Liston gamble held its collective breath. They all knew of Liston's notoriously foul temper, and they wondered what the volatile champ's reaction to this bad luck might be.

Liston picked up the dice and rolled. Snake eyes! The champ had crapped out again.

"Look at the big ugly bear," came a voice from the back of the crowd. "He can't even shoot craps."[3]

Liston recognized the voice but ignored it. He rolled again. Snake eyes again.

The hangers-on around the table fell silent. Liston stood with his back to them, tensed, waiting to hear whether that voice would have the guts to—

"Look at that big ugly bear!" repeated Cassius Clay. "He can't do nothing right!"[4]

Liston snarled, threw down the dice, and stormed over to Clay. "Listen," said Liston menacingly, "if you don't get out of here in ten seconds, I'm gonna pull that big tongue out of your mouth—"[5] And Clay walked. Later, Harold Conrad asked him whether he had been scared. "Yeah, man," Clay told Conrad, "that big ugly bear scared me bad."[6]

A few nights later, Liston brutalized Patterson, knocking him out again in the first round. Cassius Clay was one of the first people into the ring. Standing over Liston, who was sitting in his corner, Clay taunted the champ with a new poem: "Sonny Liston is great/But he'll fall in eight!"[7]

Then Clay grabbed the ring microphone. "The fight was a disgrace," he yelled into the mike. "Liston is a tramp; I'm the champ. I want that big ugly bear. I want that big bum as soon as I can get him. I'm tired of talking. If I can't whip that bum, I'll leave the country."[8]

"I was crazy then," he later recalled. "But everyone wants to believe in himself. Everybody wants to be fearless. And when people saw I had those qualities, it attracted them to me."[9]

Meanwhile, Clay's handlers had settled on a more traditional way of forcing a title bout with Liston. They signed their fighter to take on British champion Henry Cooper, the top contender outside the United States. The fight was set for London.

Clay arrived in England proclaiming, "This is no jive/ Cooper will go in five."[10] And a fifth-round knockout it was. After the fight, Clay had a welcome visitor in his dressing room—Jack Nilon, Sonny Liston's manager.

"I've flown three thousand miles just to tell you that Liston wants you," Nilon said, "You talked yourself into a world heavyweight title fight."[11] The bout was set for February 25, 1964, in Miami.

"Liston will fall in eight, 'cause I'm The Greatest!" screamed Clay at the press conference announcing the fight.[12]

"My only worry is how I'll get my fist outta his big mouth once I get him in the ring," Liston responded. "It's going to go so far down his throat it'll take a week for me to pull it out again."[13]

The oddsmakers agreed with Liston. Heavier, stronger, and more experienced, he was made a 7-1 favorite to beat Clay.

What gave Clay the courage to pursue his ambition so relentlessly? Certainly, he was naturally brash and self-assured, but perhaps he gained an extra measure of confidence from his increasing involvement with the Nation of Islam. Clay wouldn't have been the first of Liston's opponents to have taken up prayer.

Islam is a religion practiced all over the world. Its adherents, called Muslims, follow the teachings of the prophet Muhammad as proclaimed in the Koran, the Islamic equivalent of the Bible. The Nation of Islam, however, was not simply an American branch of the Muslim faith.

The Nation was founded in the 1930s by an unemployed black man in Detroit, who had been born Elijah Poole, but changed his name to Elijah Muhammad because he believed the surname Poole to be a remnant of his family's enslaved past.

Elijah Muhammad taught blacks that the white man was the devil. He preached that, for centuries, whites had used violence and deceit to subjugate blacks. And in the process, blacks had forgotten who they truly were.

According to Elijah Muhammad, in the beginning of time, all men were black. Then an evil scientist named Yacub created a race of blue-eyed, bleached devils, who used trickery to seize power and wealth and then used Christianity to keep blacks down. Still, Elijah Muhammad claimed, the day would come when the Islamic god Allah would overthrow white civilization and return blacks to their original glory.

The day-to-day behavior espoused by the Nation of Islam, however, was decidedly more sober than its mythology. Black Muslims, as members of the Nation of Islam are known, were required to renounce drugs, tobacco, alcohol, and all sex outside of marriage. They were encouraged to work hard, pursue an education, and make money. Elijah Muhammad taught his followers to take pride in their race and renounce the company of white people.

Cassius Clay first learned of the Black Muslim faith in 1959, when he picked up a Nation of Islam newspaper in Louisville. "I can still feel the powerful way [the newspaper] impressed me," he later wrote. "It was speaking out boldly against the injustice and oppression of black people, saying things that I had thought and felt, but had no one to talk to about."[14] Three years later, he met someone he could talk to: Malcolm X, the Minister of Information for the Nation of Islam.

Born Malcolm Little in 1925, Malcolm X was the son of a fiery black preacher who had been murdered by a white

Clay with Malcolm X.

mob. After moving from one foster home to another during a painful childhood, the young Malcolm became a hustler, selling dope, pimping, and running numbers for bookmakers. At the age of 20, he was sentenced to ten years in prison for a string of burglaries.

It was in prison that Malcolm was introduced and converted to the Black Muslim faith. Following Elijah Muhammad's example, Malcolm renounced his "slave name" of Little and took the name Malcolm X.

During the late 1950s, Malcolm X became the Nation of Islam's most effective proselytizer. He was both intelligent and a great public orator. "We are speaking of the collective white man's cruelties," he told his street-corner audiences. "You cannot find one black man, I do not care who he is, who has not been personally damaged by the devilish acts of the collective white man!"[15] As Malcolm X got his message out, the Nation of Islam grew rapidly. By the early 1960s, it had 15,000 registered members, at least 50,000 believers, and a much larger number of sympathizers.

For a widening segment of black America, Malcolm's voice was a source of bold, new inspiration. But for millions of white Americans, Malcolm was a despised symbol of black anger, ingratitude, and militancy—the antithesis of Martin Luther King, Jr., who believed in peaceful integration.

When Malcolm X first met Cassius Clay in Detroit in 1962, he recognized immediately that the charismatic young boxer could become an influential advocate for the Nation of Islam. "Not many people know the quality of the mind he's got in there," Malcolm told a reporter. "He fools them. One forgets that though a clown never imitates a wise man, a wise man can imitate a clown."[16]

It had taken a great deal of masquerading to keep Clay's association with the Black Muslims from becoming public knowledge. "For three years, up until I fought Sonny Liston, I'd sneak into Nation of Islam meetings through the back door," Ali later remembered. "I didn't want people to know I was there. I was afraid [that] if they knew, I wouldn't be allowed to fight for the title. Later on, I learned to stand up for my beliefs."[17]

Clay made his first public stand just before his title bout with Liston in February, 1964. He could not have asked for a better forum. Five hundred journalists had descended upon Miami, where the two fighters were training.

Most of the reporters expected to write traditional, uncontroversial boxing stories. But the complex tensions weighing on the nation at that time soon intruded when Cassius Clay invited Malcolm X to his training camp.

Rumors of Clay's involvement with the Nation of Islam were already commonplace. His cook was a Black Muslim, and so was his personal security guard. The presence of Malcolm X at Clay's camp, however, confirmed the rumors and made them public.

The promoter of the fight, Bill MacDonald, confronted Clay, demanding that he renounce the Black Muslims in public. Clay refused. Then MacDonald threatened to cancel the fight, claiming the Black Muslims' negative public image would hurt the gate and make it impossible for him to recover his investment.

It was a tense moment. The title shot that Clay had worked so hard for was on the line. Yet Clay finally shook his head. "I know I can beat Liston, and I don't want to call the fight off," he said, "but if you have to call it off because of my faith, then the fight's off."[18]

MacDonald relented. The fight went on as scheduled.

In the meantime, Clay and his friend Drew "Bundini" Brown quietly left the training camp and drove to the U.S. Army Induction Center in Coral Gables, Florida. Clay had been summoned there for physical and mental tests that would determine his draft status. At the bottom of his written examination, Clay signed his name "Cassius X."

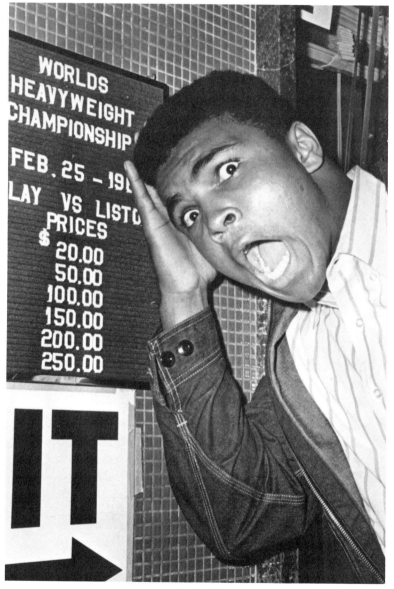

*Clay clowns for reporters before his heavyweight title bout
with Sonny Liston. "Man, I'm glad I don't have to
pay to see the fight," he joked.*

6

You'll Lose Your Money
If You Bet on Sonny

"I'm young, I'm handsome, I'm fast, I can't possibly be beat. I'm ready to go to war right now. If I see that bear in the street, I'll beat him before the fight. I'll beat him like I'm his daddy. He's too ugly to be the world champ. The world's champ should be pretty like me. If you want to lose your money, then bet on Sonny, because I'll never lose a fight. It's impossible."[1]

The weigh-in before a title fight is usually a subdued event. Mostly, photographers take pictures, and sportswriters get an easy story. With Cassius Clay, however, nothing was safe from his psychological manipulation, not even the weigh-in.

The morning of the Liston fight, Clay arrived at the weigh-in wearing a blue denim jacket; the words "Bear Huntin'" were emblazoned in red across the back. Behind him were Angelo Dundee, Sugar Ray Robinson, and his friend Bundini Brown. "Float like a butterfly, sting like a bee!" Clay was yelling. "Rumble, young man, rumble!" hollered Brown.[2]

When Clay left the room to strip, the weigh-in returned to its customary routine. Then Clay returned wearing a white robe. He stepped onto the scale, which balanced out at 210 pounds. As he stepped off, Liston arrived. Clay went wild.

"Somebody's gonna die at ringside tonight!" he raved, practically foaming at the mouth. "You scared chump! You ain't no giant! I'm going to eat you alive!"[3]

53

Members of Clay's entourage surged forward to hold back their fighter. Dr. Alexander Robbins, who was supervising the weigh-in, rushed over and took Clay's pulse. It was 110 beats per minute, more than twice its normal rate of 54. "He's emotionally imbalanced, scared to death, and liable to crack up in the ring," Robbins said. "We'll have to call the fight off if his pressure doesn't come down before he gets in that ring."[4]

Later, Angelo Dundee recalled how he restrained Clay from attacking Liston—"with one finger," Dundee said.[5] When Clay's own doctor took his pulse a few hours later, he found it to be normal. Had Clay been "scared to death?" Or was his behavior just an act to psych out Liston? Whatever the truth, Clay's outburst convinced Sonny Liston that he was about to step into the ring with a crazy man.

During the first round, the two fighters felt each other out. Clay landed a few combinations; Liston connected with a hard right to Clay's stomach. When the bell sounded to end

Clay connects with a left to Liston's eye.

the round, Clay skipped back to his corner, while Liston purposefully strode over to his. At least Clay had shown that he could survive one round with Liston, which was more than Floyd Patterson had done.

In the second round, Liston momentarily trapped Clay against the ropes and landed a solid left hook to the head. The crowd had been screaming since the opening bell, but the shouting got even louder as Liston appeared ready to finish off the upstart. But then Clay shook off the punch, escaped from the ropes, and finished the round dancing.

In the third round, Clay took control. He took the fight to Liston and landed a hard one-two combination. Liston's right cheek began to swell, and a nasty gash opened up over his left eye. For the first time in his boxing career, Liston had been cut.

Then, just as Clay could taste victory, he almost lost it all. Clay had cruised through most of the fourth round, avoiding Liston's blows and landing quick punches of his own, when some liniment, an anti-irritant cream, from Liston's shoulder somehow got into Clay's eyes, causing them to burn and sting. The liniment temporarily blinded him. "I can't see!" Clay screamed as he stumbled back to his corner at the end of the round. "Cut the gloves off!" he yelled at Dundee. "We're going home!"[6]

Dundee would have none of it. He cleaned out Clay's eyes as best he could, and as the bell rang to open the fifth, he shoved his fighter back into the ring. Dancing and keeping Liston at arm's length, Clay managed to survive until his vision cleared. Then, once more, he snapped punches into Liston's face.

Liston limped back to his corner at the end of the sixth round. He had trained for only a three-round fight, having assumed that he would knock Clay out quickly. But now those three rounds were history. Liston's face was bleeding, he was feeling the effects of bursitis in his shoulder—making every punch agony—and Clay showed no signs of tiring.

The champ knew that he had already lost too many rounds to have any real chance of winning the fight by decision. Liston also knew that, as things stood, it was not he but Clay who seemed most likely to win by a knockout. "Liston is great/But he'll fall in eight!"[7] the challenger had predicted. The thought of an eighth-round knockout actually coming to pass must have weighed heavily on Liston's mind between rounds six and seven.

When the bell rang for the seventh round, Liston stayed slumped in his corner. He refused to come out. The fight was over. Cassius Clay was the new heavyweight champion.

In his ecstasy, Clay leaped into the air, then rushed to the press section and shook a gloved fist at the reporters who had written that he'd be destroyed by Liston. "EAT YOUR WORDS!" he yelled. "I TOLD YOU I WAS THE GREATEST. I AM SO GREAT! I...AM...THE...GREATEST!"[8]

The next day, Clay held an unnaturally subdued press conference, his first as champion. "He was so unusually soft-spoken," one reporter remembered, "that we had to strain to hear him."[9] What Clay had to say, though, made loud headlines.

In response to questions about his rumored involvement with the Black Muslims, Clay finally admitted that he had indeed joined the Nation of Islam. He announced that he was disowning his "slave name" of Clay and from then on wished to be known as Cassius X.

The reporters at the press conference were shocked. Even though they had been asking the questions, few had anticipated the new champion's answers. As far as most Americans were concerned, the Nation of Islam was a gang of violent militants who preached a gospel of hate. And the reporters were used to fighters telling them only how much they weighed and what they ate while they were training.

"I know where I'm going and I know the truth and I don't have to be what you want me to be," Cassius X said. "I'm free to be who I want."[10]

"Where do you think I'd be next week," he asked the reporters, "if I didn't know how to shout and holler and make the public take notice? I'd be poor and I'd probably be in my home town, washing windows or running an elevator and saying, 'yes suh' and 'no suh' and knowing my place. Instead of that, I'm one of the highest paid athletes in the world. Think about that. A southern colored boy has made one million dollars."[11]

A month later, the champ held another press conference and this time announced that his new Islamic name would be Muhammad Ali. He told the reporters that he had been given the name by Elijah Muhammad himself, because it meant "worthy of praise most high."

Ali's press conference generated a lot of publicity, but it would be a long time before the media would come to accept his new name and identity. *The New York Times*, for instance, maintained for many years a typical editorial policy. The first time the champ was mentioned in a story, he was "Cassius Clay, who prefers to be known as Muhammad Ali." Subsequently, he was referred to as Clay.

Over the next few months, Ali divided his time between Chicago, the headquarters of the Nation of Islam, and Harlem, where Malcolm X was based. In Chicago, Elijah's son, Herbert Muhammad, introduced Ali to Sonji Roi, a beautiful cocktail waitress and model. She was a year older than Ali and had an eight-year-old son from a previous marriage. Ali fell in love with her, and they married.

But the marriage lasted less than a year, because Roi refused to adhere to the strict Muslim dress and dining codes. Although he said he still loved her, Ali divorced Roi rather than have his religious devotion compromised.

During the short time they were married, Ali and Roi made a tour of northern Africa during which Ali met with such illustrious Muslim leaders as Kwame Nkrumah of Ghana and Gamal Abdel Nasser of Egypt. They told him of the support he had throughout the Islamic world. "He was the first world champion to actually have a world to be champion of," one observer wrote.[12]

This support, however, did not extend to mainstream white America, which was both angry with and frightened by the Nation of Islam. White Americans at the time were increasingly concerned with the possibility of riots in black urban ghettos. Many whites believed that groups such as the Black Muslims were fomenting violent unrest through speeches and writings that encouraged blacks to stand up against white society. These critics often refused to recognize that horrific inner city conditions might be the underlying cause of black indignation.

As a conspicuous member of the Nation of Islam, Ali often found himself the target of attacks on the Nation of Islam. In an editorial entitled "Boxing's Feet of Clay," for example, the *Saturday Evening Post* took its own swipe at Ali:

If Cassius Clay fights Sonny Liston again, which one would you root for?… It is easy to be against Sonny until you consider the record of Cassius Clay. For a

Ali addresses a Black Muslim convention in Chicago.

time, when he was confining himself to bad poetry, Cassius was a loudmouth but a likable character who seemed harmless.... After the fight he acknowledged that he was a Black Muslim, converted by the arch-extremist, Malcolm X....

As we were saying, a Clay-Liston rematch would be a tough choice. It boils down to a question of whether you prefer your violence on an individual or organized basis....[13]

An Ali-Liston rematch was scheduled for May 25, 1965. Originally, the fight was set for Boston, but it was later switched to a high school hockey rink in Lewiston, Maine—the Massachusetts boxing commissioners having decided that they didn't want their state tainted by the publicity surrounding two such louts as Liston and Ali.

Meanwhile, on August 2, 1964, as Ali and Liston trained for their rematch, the Pentagon reported that North Vietnamese patrol boats had attacked an American destroyer in the Gulf of Tonkin, off the coast of Vietnam. President Lyndon Johnson used the alleged attack to rally public support for his policy of escalating the war there. He demanded that Congress approve a resolution giving him virtually unlimited authority to use any means necessary to defeat the Communist North. Congress approved the resolution overwhelmingly on August 7.

After winning reelection in November, Johnson ordered a dramatic expansion of the bombing of North Vietnam. This necessitated the stationing of additional American bomber groups in South Vietnam, which in turn required extra troops to protect them. By the end of 1965, there were 180,000 American servicemen in country. More were expected. At home, the draft was expanded to keep up with the increasing demand for fresh soldiers.

But Muhammad had other things on his mind when he stepped into the ring to face Sonny Liston a second time. As though Liston himself weren't enough to worry about, there had been threats made on Ali's life, and it was rumored that an assassin would be stalking him from somewhere in the arena.

In the months following Ali's conversion, the Nation of Islam had been torn by a split between Malcolm X and his one-time mentor, Elijah Muhammad. Malcolm's faith had been shaken when he discovered that Elijah Muhammad had been guilty of sexual misconduct with several of his secretaries. The two argued privately until on March 12, 1964, Malcolm finally announced that he had split with the Nation of Islam. Two months later, after an extended trip to Africa, Malcolm revealed plans for the formations of a new group, the Organization for Afro-American Unity.

After he parted from the Nation of Islam, Malcolm backed off of a number of his more extremist views. While he still rejected Martin Luther King's vision of peaceful, gradual integration, Malcolm nevertheless realized that accommodations with whites would have to be made, that strength alone was not enough. Before he could fully articulate these new views, however, Malcolm was silenced. He was shot to death at the Audubon Ballroom in New York City on February 21, 1965. The alleged gunmen were all members of the Nation of Islam.

No one is absolutely sure who ordered the killing of Malcolm X, but it was widely assumed that Elijah Muhammad was responsible, and that sooner or later Malcolm's followers would take revenge. Because Ali was still loyal to Elijah Muhammad and the Nation of Islam, many people thought

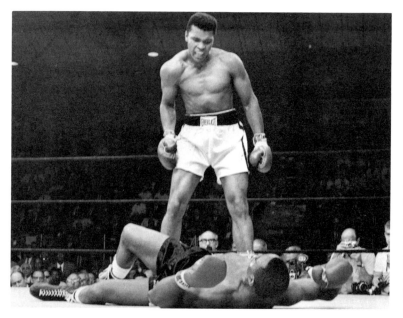

Ali stands over Liston after his first-round knockout.

he might be a prime candidate for such an attack. Even the FBI sent agents to guard Ali's training camp as he prepared for his second fight with Liston.

Given the extravagant headlines that preceded it, Ali-Liston II was something of an anticlimax. The 2,434 fans, who had braved both the rumors of mayhem and the searches of guards, were only just settling into their seats when the fight was over. "It was either the most sensational heavyweight championship of all time, or the most disgraceful affair ever to masquerade as a title fight," one reporter wrote.[14]

In the opening round, Ali threw a seemingly innocuous punch that looked as though it barely grazed Liston's temple. "I saw the punch, and it wouldn't have crushed a grape," one veteran fight writer insisted.[15] Yet there was Liston, lying crumpled on the canvas as Ali stood over him, screaming

"Get up! Get up and fight!" Liston stayed down as the referee counted him out. Ali had won again, an unbelievable first-round knockout.

Critics charged that the fight had been fixed, calling Ali's blow the Phantom Punch." At least one ringside reporter, however, saw it differently: "The fighters were moving toward each other at top speed, each throwing his weight of more than two hundred pounds behind a potential knockout punch. Liston's, a left, missed. Ali's, a short right thrown on a downward arc, smashed into the left side of Liston's face. The challenger collapsed slowly, like a building crumbling during an earthquake."[16]

In the wake of Ali's remarkable defense of the heavyweight title, the public cried out for a challenger who could take on Ali. Fifty years before, people had begged for a "Great White Hope" to beat Jack Johnson. After the second Liston fight, Ali's detractors would have accepted anybody, black or white, who could silence this Black Muslim. An aging Floyd Patterson, himself a two-time loser to Liston, stepped forward. A fight between Ali and Patterson, a follower of Dr. King, was scheduled for November 22, 1965.

"I say it, and I say it flatly, that the image of a Black Muslim as the world heavyweight champion disgraces the sport and the nation," Patterson asserted. "Cassius Clay must be beaten and the Black Muslims' scourge removed from boxing."[17]

For his part, Ali claimed that he would not attack Patterson personally, politically, or spiritually. But his performance in the ring was the more decisive statement. Ali so single-mindedly punished Floyd Patterson that one reporter likened the fight to a small boy torturing a butterfly. Ali carried Patterson for twelve rounds, peppering him with jabs and taunting him for his disparagement of Ali's religious views. The referee finally stopped the fight when it was apparent that Patterson was being hurt beyond human endurance.

Before the fight, Patterson had intentionally referred to the champ as Cassius Clay. Facing the press after the fight, Patterson graciously admitted, "I was beaten by a great fighter, Muhammad Ali."[18]

7

Drafted

During the Vietnam War, young men were required to register on their eighteenth birthdays with the Selective Service System, otherwise known as the draft board. Those considered fit were given draft cards. On each card was a number. Selective Service periodically held lotteries. If your number came up, you were drafted.

To determine which young men were fit for military service, all potential draftees underwent a series of physical, intellectual, and psychological tests. Those who passed became eligible for the draft lottery. Selective Service classified every young man of draft age according to his performance on these tests. The classifications were: 1A, or fit for duty; 1Y, or below physical or mental standards; 2S, a deferment given to college students; and 4F, or unfit for duty. When the number of a 1A came up, he was ordered to report for a final round of tests. If he passed them, he was immediately inducted into the armed forces and sent off to boot camp. From there, it was quite likely that he would be sent to Vietnam.

Muhammad Ali took a second series of Selective Service tests in March, 1964, shortly after winning the title from Liston. The results of the first set he had taken in Florida before the fight had been deemed inconclusive. This time, Ali failed one of the written tests. "I said I was the Greatest, not the smartest," he joked after being declared 1Y.[1]

Almost two years later, on February 17, 1966, Ali was in Miami, training for a March defense of his title against Ernie

"The Octopus" Terrell, set for Comiskey Park in Chicago. A reporter called the champ at his North Miami home. He wanted to know Ali's reaction to the news that Selective Service had just reclassified him from 1Y to 1A, or fit for duty.

Ali was outraged. "How can they do this without another test to see if I'm any wiser...than last time?" he said.[2] Later that day, Ali held an impromptu press conference. "I've got a question," Ali told the reporters. "For two years the Government caused me international embarrassment, letting people think I was a nut...and now they jump up and make me 1A without even an official notification or a test. Why did they let me be considered a nut, an illiterate, for two years?"[3]

The truth was, Selective Service had changed the standards for everyone. More troops were needed for the widening war in Vietnam, so standards were lowered across the board. Ali just happened to be the most famous young man to be reclassified.

Reporters followed up with questions about Ali's own opinion of the war. Ali confessed that he wasn't even sure where Vietnam was. They pressed him. Did he really want South Vietnam to fall to the Vietcong, the communist guerrillas supported by North Vietnam? Ali shrugged. "I ain't got no quarrel with them Vietcong," he said.[4]

For the previous twelve years, Vietnam had been engaged in a civil war. Vietnamese nationalists led by Ho Chi Minh had defeated the colonial French forces at Dien Bien Phu in 1954. At the peace conference following the French surrender, it was agreed that the country would be temporarily divided into a northern sector controlled by a communist government under Ho and a southern sector controlled by Vietnamese Catholics backed by the United States. The peace treaty also called for an election to reunite the country, but that election—which would unquestionably have been won by Ho—was never held. Instead, the Republic of South Vietnam, with American encouragement, declared itself an independent nation.

The United States at that time was bent on containing the spread of communism. So when Vietcong rebels in the south began taking up arms against the South Vietnamese government, the Americans sent economic and military aid, including advisors, munitions, and eventually ground troops. And when American planes began bombing North Vietnam, which was supplying the Vietcong, the North Vietnamese army entered the fight.

Ali's conversion to the Nation of Islam had upset many people, but not as many as were infuriated by his stance on Vietnam. In 1966, protest against the war was still in its early stages. The only real public dissent was coming from radical students and sympathetic professors. Public opinion was overwhelmingly against them. Polls showed that most people, although they didn't support the war, at least accepted it.

A firestorm of controversy engulfed Ali in the days following his press conference. He was inundated with threatening phone calls, hostile letters, and vindictive telegrams. "YOU HAVE DISGRACED YOUR TITLE AND THE AMERICAN FLAG AND THE PRINCIPLES FOR WHICH IT STANDS," read a telegram from former heavyweight champ Gene Tunney. "APOLOGIZE FOR YOUR UNPATRIOTIC REMARK OR YOU'LL BE BARRED FROM THE RING."[5]

Though he soon realized that more was at stake than just public relations, Ali refused to back down. Then came the ultimatum: The Illinois Athletic Commission demanded that Ali publicly apologize for his remarks or else his Chicago fight with Terrell would be cancelled.

In retrospect, the commission's position was absurd. The sole responsibility of a state athletic commission was to ensure that the boxers it licensed were physically able to withstand the punishment of the ring. It was not up to a commission to tell fighters what to think. "I'm not sure exactly why the Illinois Athletic Commission felt that it was the proper body to accept an apology from Ali," Angelo Dundee noted sarcastically. "But then reason didn't have much to do with the attitude toward Ali at the time."[6]

Appearing before the commission, Ali apologized for having made the remarks publicly to reporters before notifying the proper authorities of his position. But he refused to apologize for the content of what he said. The fight with Terrell was promptly cancelled.

For the next few months, no state athletic commission would sanction a bout involving Ali, so between March and September of 1966, Ali had to schedule all four of his fights outside the United States, in Canada and Europe. These were also the last fights covered by his agreement with the Louisville Sponsoring Group. From that point on, Ali turned over his business affairs to Elijah Muhammad's son, Herbert.

In the fall of 1966, public opinion against Ali softened somewhat. Texas and New York both sanctioned him to fight, and his next three title defenses took place in these states. He would not fight again, however, for three years.

By early 1967, American planes were dropping about 825 tons of bombs each day on North Vietnam, a country the size of the state of Washington. In an attempt to deny communist soldiers food and shelter, the United States was destroying millions of acres of crops and forest land. By the war's end, eighteen million gallons of the extremely toxic herbicide Agent Orange would be sprayed on South Vietnam alone.

The ordeal of Vietnam takes its toll on this American soldier.

Muhammad Ali was determined to have nothing to do with this war. Not only did he have "no quarrel" with the Viet-cong, he believed his devotion to Islam mandated pacifism.

Late in the winter of 1967, he received a notice to appear before the draft board in Houston, Texas, on April 28. His number had come up, and the heavyweight champion of the world was to be inducted into the armed forces. On April 25, he met with reporters at a coffee shop in Chicago. They asked him whether he would go along with the draft. He said no. Then they asked him why not. Surely he would only be asked to fight exhibitions for the troops, as Joe Louis had during World War II. Journalist Robert Lipsyte recorded Ali's response:

What can you give me, America, for turning down my religion? How can I lose for standing up for Islam when presidents and princes invite me to their

69

countries, when little people all over the East and Africa stop me in the street and say "Eat at my house, brother, be an honor if you stay with us, brother?"

You want me to give up all this love, America? You want me to do what the white man says and go fight a war against some people I don't know nothing about—get some freedom for some other people when my own people can't get theirs here?

You want me to be so scared of the white man I'll go and get two arms shot off and 10 medals so you can give me a small salary and pat my head and say, "Good boy, he fought for his country?" Every day, they die in Vietnam for nothing. I might as well die right here for something.[7]

On April 28, when Ali refused to step forward at the Houston induction center, every boxing organization stripped him of his title. Every state athletic commission revoked his license to fight. The Justice Department had him indicted on a felony charge for his refusal to submit to induction, and the State Department revoked his passport. His case, *United States of America v. Cassius Marsellus Clay*, began its four-year journey through the courts. (His middle name was misspelled on the docket because Ali himself had misspelled it on the Selective Service questionnaire.) In the meantime, Muhammad Ali could not box in the United States. And because he had no passport, he couldn't leave the country to fight elsewhere.

"I'm not in any position to say what was right and what was wrong about his stand on the draft," Angelo Dundee said. "All I know is that he was sincere about it and that it cost him a heck of a lot more to stick with what he believes than it will ever cost most men."[8]

8

Exile and Return

On June 20, 1967, Muhammad Ali was convicted of "refusing to be inducted." The judge gave him the maximum al-
lowable sentence: five years in prison and a $10,000 fine.
Through a series of appeals, Ali's lawyers managed to keep
him out of jail. His case would eventually reach the Supreme
Court.

On August 17, 1967, Ali married for the second time. His
new wife, Belinda Boyd, was a seventeen-year-old Black
Muslim from Chicago. On June 18, 1968, she gave birth to
their first child, a girl the couple named Maryum. Two years
later, the Alis had twins, Jamillah and Rasheda. Muhammad,
Jr., was born in 1972.

During the three-and-a-half years of his exile from the
ring, Ali supported himself and his family in a variety of
ways, including appearances on college campuses. Ali's prepared speeches on "The Intoxication of Fame" and "Friend-
ship and Self-Interest" enthralled his young audiences, but
they really came to life during the lively question-and-answer
sessions. "I ain't the Greatest no more because Allah is the
Greatest. But I'm still the prettiest!" Ali would say.[1]

Ali also acted in a Broadway show called *Buck White*, and
he began writing an autobiography. But Ali was no lecturer,
actor, or writer, and he knew it. He belonged in the ring, and
those years he lost, from ages 25 to 29, should have been his
prime as a boxer. He could only watch as Jimmy Ellis, a former sparring partner, took the title and then lost it in Febru-

ary, 1970, to a crude but powerful puncher, "Smokin'" Joe Frazier. The only people Ali could fight were the state athletic commissioners, to whom he constantly appealed for reinstatement.

Meanwhile, in Vietnam, the war dragged on despite General Westmoreland's repeated assurances that the end was in sight. All that changed on January 30, 1968, when the Vietcong launched a massive surprise attack during the Asian holiday of Tet. Although the communists suffered enormous losses and a clear military defeat, the fact that they were able to bring such force to bear, even breaching the U.S. embassy compound in Saigon, had a devastating effect on domestic public opinion. The Tet Offensive, as it came to be known, made it clear that the war, while still perhaps winnable, would surely not be over soon.

College students had been opposing the war in large numbers for a few years, but now many of their parents joined the protests. In March, 1968, President Lyndon Johnson nearly lost the New Hampshire primary to Senator Eugene McCarthy, who was running on an antiwar platform. Clearly, public support for Johnson and his Vietnam policy had eroded dramatically. Three weeks later, in a nationally televised speech, President Johnson announced that he was ordering a reduction in the bombing of North Vietnam in order to stimulate stalled peace talks, and that he would not seek reelection for a second term.

After Johnson bowed out, the race for the Democratic nomination narrowed to two candidates—Senator Robert Kennedy, the late president's brother, who was perceived as an antiwar candidate, and Vice President Hubert Humphrey, who had antiwar sympathies but remained firmly associated, at least in the public mind, with the policies of the Johnson

Demonstrators protest America's involvement in the Vietnam War

Administration. The night Kennedy won the California pri-mary, however, he was shot to death in Los Angeles, just one month after Martin Luther King, Jr., had been assassinated in Memphis.

The violence continued through the rest of the summer of 1968, and both political conventions were marred by riots and angry protests. Black neighborhoods in North Miami burned as the Republican Party nominated Richard Nixon in Miami Beach. In Chicago, thousands of demonstrators were beaten by police outside the convention hall where Hubert Humphrey was nominated. Some observers worried that America was on the brink of a second Civil War.

Given this climate, a young man, Black Muslim or not, who said, "I ain't got nothing against them Vietcong" no longer seemed disloyal. Muhammad Ali hadn't compromised one bit. Instead, Americans, by and large, had come to agree with him.

As 1969 and 1970 passed, Ali's professional status was gradually restored. On September 28, 1970, a federal judge in New York authorized the renewal of Ali's boxing license in that state. The license had originally been revoked on moral grounds. But the judge found that this standard was inconsistently and therefore unfairly applied. Convicted robbers, rapists, and even army deserters all held licenses to fight in New York state. If those criminals were considered moral enough to box, the judge concluded, why should Muhammad Ali be singled out for "conduct detrimental to the sport?" Later that fall, black state legislators in Georgia managed to have a fight sanctioned between Ali and a respected white contender, Jerry Quarry.

Ali's comeback was set for October 26, but Georgia governor Lester Maddox, an outspoken segregationist, tried to block it. When he failed, he declared October 26 a statewide "Day of Mourning." But it was a day of mourning only for Quarry, whom Ali cut badly enough in the third round to end the fight in a technical knockout, or TKO. Next came Oscar Bonavena, the Argentinean champ, in December, 1970. Ali knocked him out in the fifteenth round.

In each of these fights, however, Ali showed signs of the negative effect of the layoff. Some of it was rustiness, but he had also lost some of his quickness and his punches seemed to have less sting. Still, Ali had knocked out Bonavena, while the current champion, Joe Frazier, had only managed a decision. In the ring immediately after the Bonavena fight, Ali grabbed the microphone from television broadcaster Howard Cosell and looked straight into the cameras. "I have done what Joe Frazier couldn't do!" he shouted. "I have knocked out Oscar Bonavena! Now where is he? I want Frazier!!!"[2] Ali was definitely back, but was he still the Greatest?

A fight with Frazier was scheduled for March 8, 1971, in Madison Square Garden. Soon it came to be known as The Fight. "It's the greatest event in the history of the world," Ali announced.[3]

What boxing fan could have asked for more? Two undefeated champions facing off against each other. This had never happened before in the history of boxing, and the hype notwithstanding, it was widely expected to be one of the greatest nights in the history of sports and likely the greatest fight ever.

Frazier and Ali were a perfect match. Ali was the dancer, the artist, who finessed his opponents with quick jabs to the head; Frazier was a bull, a body puncher, who relied on his power to bludgeon his challengers.

The two fighters also had sharply different personalities. Ali was flamboyant, egotistical, and controversial. Frazier, however—like Liston—was quiet and contemplative. He planned to become a preacher after his retirement from the ring. As a result of this sharp contrast, The Fight took on symbolic significance.

Though by no means an apologist for whites, Frazier was cast as the defender of the old order, the man who would finally put the "uppity" Ali in his place. Ali, however, had his own supporters among those who identified with the protests and social experimentation of the 1960s. To these people, a victory by Ali would provide symbolic redemption for all the countless individuals who had been crushed by the "Establishment." Novelist Norman Mailer wrote that Ali "was the mightiest victim of injustice in the land. Every...plain, simple individualist adored him."[4]

To the boxers themselves, The Fight was a matter of pride. Only one of them could be champ. It didn't escape notice, however, that The Fight would be an unprecedented financial bonanza. Ali and Frazier would split an incredible $5 million purse, at a time when a newspaper still cost a dime and a new car no more than a few thousand dollars. Each fighter would make $2,500,000, win, lose, or draw. Copies of the signed checks were published in newspapers the day of the fight. Ali's share was more than his combined earnings from his first twenty-seven pro fights, which included eight title bouts. The promoters felt they had made a safe investment, however, because millions more would be made through a closed-circuit broadcast of the fight. The Wall Street Journal estimated that total revenues would exceed $40 million.

How did the two fighters respond to this pressure? Ali trained—but not as hard as he might have. His three-and-a-half years of exile seemed to have blunted his capacity for grueling preparation. He ran three miles a day when he could have run five. Some days he sparred; others, he didn't. Meanwhile, Frazier was training as he had never trained before. In comparison, Ali's approach to the fight was almost casual.

The bout itself was anything but casual, though. Madison Square Garden was packed, with $150 ringside seats fetching five times that price from scalpers; 350 theaters across the United States and Canada, as well as thirty-three in England, showed the closed-circuit broadcast; another thirty countries tuned in via satellite. The whole world was watching.

Frazier came out "smokin'," battering Ali with right jabs and a powerful left hook. But Ali confounded expectations. Instead of giving Frazier dancing lessons, Ali stood toe-to-toe with him. His strategy seemed to be to absorb all the punishment Frazier could dish out, then outslug the slugger.

Ali dominated the early rounds, beating Frazier's head until his features began to swell beyond recognition. But in the middle rounds, Ali tired. He spent more and more time on the ropes, where he couldn't dodge Frazier's furious body punches. Yet Ali didn't concede a thing. Throughout the beating, Ali shook his head as if to say, "You're not hurting me.... That didn't hurt." In return, he lashed out with blows to Frazier's face.

As the fight went on, Ali's strategy took its toll on Frazier, whose face became scarred and bloody. In the eleventh round, however, Frazier connected with a vicious left hook to the jaw that hurt Ali. In the rounds that followed, Ali's jaw swelled considerably, and Frazier poured it on, looking for the knockout. Badly hurt himself, Frazier churned away at Ali with one body blow after another. Frazier's superior training and

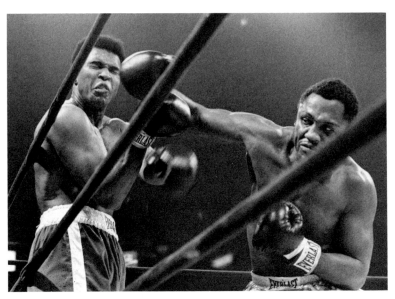

Frazier stuns Ali with a blow to the head during their first fight in Madison Square Garden.

younger legs were making a noticeable difference. He was able to take Ali's best punches and still keep coming. There was a reason Smokin' Joe was the champ.

In the fourteenth round, Ali dug deep inside himself and found the strength for one last rally. He won the round with a late flurry and came out for the fifteenth looking like the Ali of old, dancing and peppering Frazier with jabs. And then—for an instant—Ali lowered his guard. Frazier threw a perfect left hook, again to the jaw, and Ali went down. For the first time in nine years, Ali went down. Frazier stood over him, breathing heavily.

Ali got back up, but for the last two minutes and thirty-five seconds of the fight, he stumbled around in a daze, barely able to keep Frazier at arm's length. Somehow, he made it through to the bell. Then he slumped into his corner, impassive and expressionless. Moments later, the unanimous decision was announced: Joe Frazier had retained the heavyweight title. The crowd exploded.

Beaten for the first time in his professional career, Ali was turning to leave the ring when he felt a tug on the sleeve of his robe. It was Frazier, his face so swollen that Ali could barely see his eyes.

"You put up a great fight," said Frazier.

"You the Champ," said Ali.

The next day, Ali held a press conference. He seemed calm and self-assured. "Just lost a fight, that's all," he told reporters. "More important things to worry about in life. Probably a better man for it."[5]

But the reporters wouldn't let him off so graciously. One reminded Ali of his first fight with Liston when he'd promised that if he lost, he'd be on the street the next day hollering, "No man ever beat me twice."

A smile slowly spread across Ali's battered face. "I remember," he said. "And do you know what I say now? Get me Joe Frazier. No man ever beat me twice!"

Ali began to warm to the act. "I'll get by Joe this time," he continued, his voice rising in mock anger. "I'll straighten this out! I'm ready this time! Joe, you hear me? Joe, if you beat me this time you'll really be the greatest!!!"[6]

Joe Frazier didn't hear Ali. He was in the hospital, recuperating. He'd stay there for the next three weeks.

9

Ali, Bomaye!

On June 28, 1971, Ali was in Chicago, training for his next fight a month later against Jimmy Ellis. That afternoon, the Supreme Court handed down its verdict in the case *United States of America v. Cassius Marsellus Clay*. By a unanimous decision, the Court found Ali not guilty because he was sincere in his religious beliefs and could not be forced by the government to compromise them.

"Ali had won the biggest fight he would ever fight," his friend Howard Cosell wrote. "...But nobody could give him back the three and a half years that had been taken from him. Nobody."[1]

Beginning with the Ellis bout, Ali fought a series of tune-ups designed to get him back in shape for a rematch with Frazier. From July, 1971, through February, 1973, Ali fought ten times, challenging nearly every heavyweight contender he could find, including Floyd Patterson, world light-heavyweight champion Bob Foster, and Jerry Quarry. Ali beat them all. The purses ranged from $200,000 to $500,000, unprecedented amounts for non-title fights. The robe that Ali wore during this time, a gift from Elvis Presley, proclaimed him, "The People's Champion." A Frazier-Ali title rematch seemed inevitable.

But, as usual, things did not go smoothly for Ali. His plans for a rematch against Frazier ended on January 22, 1973, when George Foreman knocked out the champ and took the title. Like Ali and Frazier, Foreman was an Olympic gold medal winner, but physically he was more imposing than either, combining the height and reach of Ali with the physique and raw power of Liston. Furthermore, he had ring savvy.

The Frazier-Foreman fight seemed like a replay of Patterson-Liston. Frazier came out swinging, confident of an easy victory, but he ran into a wall. While Ali had been unable to put Frazier on the canvas, Foreman scored six knockdowns in less than two rounds before the referee stopped the fight. Frazier sat, stunned, as Foreman strode back to his corner like a man who'd just finished another routine day at the office.

Then, on March 31, Ali's dream of recapturing the title suffered another—seemingly insurmountable—setback. That day he fought a promising young Californian named Ken Norton, who had once sparred with Frazier but wasn't considered a serious threat to Ali. In fact, the fight had originally been scheduled as a final light workout before a rematch with Frazier.

Ali was still not in the best of shape, however, and early in the fight Norton connected with a hard punch to the face, breaking Ali's jaw. Ali managed to gut out the pain and go the distance, but the agony of boxing with a broken jaw put him at a severe disadvantage. Norton won in a split decision, and suddenly Ali was twice-beaten. At 31 years old, with much of his fabled quickness just a memory, "The Greatest" looked to some like a faded has-been.

After the Norton fight, Ali received an anonymous message scrawled on the back of a brown paper bag. It read: "The butterfly has lost its wings. The bee has lost its sting. You are through, you loud-mouthed braggart. Your mouth has been shut up for all times. It's a great day for America. You are finished."[2] Ali taped the bag onto the wall of his gym so he could see it every day. As soon as his jaw healed, Ali began training again. He had some scores to settle. First, Ali fought a rematch with Norton in September, 1973, winning a close but unanimous decision. Then, on January 28, 1974, he fought his long awaited rematch with Frazier, again in Madison Square Garden, the mecca of boxing.

Although this time neither man held the heavyweight title, Frazier and Ali fought with a ferocity fueled by personal animosity. Frazier had expected, after the first fight, that a victory in the ring would bring him acceptance. But Ali's popularity and status outside the ring was such that, even in defeat, the darling of the media could still crow about his greatness. Frazier didn't feel that he'd been treated as a true champion, and he blamed that entirely on Ali.

The dislike, however, didn't preclude a mutual respect. "We were gladiators," Frazier remembered. "I didn't ask no favors of him, and he didn't ask none of me. I don't like [Ali], but I got to say, inside the ring he was a man."[3]

That night Ali displayed flashes of his once nimble footwork and blinding hand speed. Avoiding the ropes, Ali danced this time, tied Frazier up when he got too close, and jabbed incessantly. He never knocked Joe Frazier down, but he didn't have to, winning a twelve-round unanimous decision. Immediately, Frazier called for a rematch, and while Ali said he wasn't going to duck Joe, he was making other plans. A few months later, Ali signed to fight Foreman.

Since winning the title from Frazier, George Foreman had fought only two bouts. He erased Joe Roman in one round and disposed of Ken Norton in two. Three title fights, five rounds, an even dozen knockdowns. As Liston had, Foreman seemed invincible, overwhelmingly powerful. The only thing that still separated Foreman from the undisputed title of greatest heavyweight alive was the shadow of Ali. Foreman knew that he would have to beat Muhammad Ali to be considered the true champion. Oddsmakers made Foreman a 3-1 favorite.

The fight was set for October 30, 1974, in a soccer stadium in Kinshasa, Zaire, one of central Africa's newly independent nations. The country had been a Belgian colony before gaining its independence during the period of decolonization following World War II. Its leader was the fiercely nationalistic President Mobutu Sese Seko. Ali and Foreman deliberately chose to fight in Zaire because their title bout would create a great deal of revenue for the government through ticket sales and tourism, as well as bringing international attention to the fledgling nation.

Ali was pleased to have the fight staged in Africa. He called it "The Rumble in the Jungle." Ali's popularity during this time was at an all-time high. His years of exile and struggle had brought him great sympathy, while people's strong interest in his self-promotional antics had never abated. Mil-

Ali is mobbed by fans in Kinshasa, Zaire.

lions of fans the world over now laughed with him instead of at him. Another title shot for Ali this late in his career, more than a decade after he first won the heavyweight championship, fired the imagination of the public, even more so than his first fight with Frazier had. And this would be an even bigger payday. Each fighter was guaranteed to receive no less than $5 million.

Foreman and Ali both trained in Zaire. Working harder than he had in years, Ali sparred with Larry Holmes, himself a future heavyweight champion, and pushed himself to the limits of his endurance. Still, hard work did not prevent Ali from issuing his customary barrage of taunts. "They think [Foreman's] going to beat me?" Ali screamed at reporters. "He can't hit!... He's got slow punches, take a year to get there. You think that's going to bother me?"[4]

For his part, Foreman remained unmoved by Ali's bluster. Other fighters from Liston to Frazier had been exasperated, embarrassed, and angered by Ali's psychological warfare. But George Foreman just smiled. "He makes me think of a parrot who keeps saying `You're stupid, you're stupid,'" Foreman told reporters. "Not to offend Muhammad Ali, but he's like that parrot. What he says, he's said before."[5]

The fight was scheduled to begin at 4:00 A.M., Kinshasa time, so that it could take place in prime time in the United States. Although it was hours before dawn, the temperature hovered at a humid 90 degrees. As Ali warmed up before the fight, Angelo Dundee handed him a copy of the *Chicago Tribune*. The headline read, "ALI NEEDS A MIRACLE TO SURVIVE."[6] Ali just nodded. He had worked hard enough to believe in miracles.

As Ali trotted into the ring beneath a waning African moon, the crowd of 70,000 left no doubt as to whom they favored. "Ali, bomaye!" they chanted, "Ali, bomaye!" which translates as "Kill him, Ali." Bundini Brown leaned over and told Ali, "Remember what I said. God set it up this way. This is the closing of the book. The king gained his throne by killing a monster, and the king will regain his throne by killing a bigger monster. This is the closing of the book."[7]

As the twenty-five-year-old Foreman stood beside the thirty-two-year-old Ali waiting for the opening bell, Ali stared into the champ's eyes. "You've heard of me since you were young," he told Foreman. "You've been following me since you were a little boy. Now, you must face me, your master!"[8]

Foreman moved purposefully into the middle of the ring. And Ali—Ali the dancer, the nimble Ali—came right at him and met him with a right lead. *A right lead?* "Champions do not hit other champions with right-hand leads," wrote one boxing expert after the fight.[9] The right lead is one of the most difficult and dangerous punches because it leaves the puncher wide open to a retaliatory hard cross.

Ali's opening punch was a warning. It told Foreman that he was not intimidated and not afraid. Foreman was outraged. He responded with a furious barrage of blows. But Ali's defense was brilliant. He used his arms and gloves to absorb Foreman's body punches, then fought back with short left jabs to Foreman's head. The first rounds were scored even. Then, during the middle rounds, the heat and Foreman's pounding seemed to hurt Ali as he spent more and more time covered up on the ropes, absorbing Foreman's punishment. But Foreman also began to slow down. The champion's punches grew clumsier, and his breathing became heavy as he began to lumber.

By the eighth round, it seemed as though anything could happen. Ali sagged on the ropes, his shoulders drooping and his arms hanging down. Foreman was exhausted, trembling with rage and frustration. He lunged at Ali but was unable to land the punch that would knock the older man out. And then, with twenty seconds left in the round, Ali sprung off the ropes. He skipped into the center of the ring, moving like the Ali of 1960. Foreman followed. He threw a long left, which Ali ducked and countered with a right cross. Foreman knew he was in trouble. He was stepping back, struggling to regain his defense, when Ali hit him.

There was never any doubt about this punch. There was nothing "phantom" about it. Somehow, the exhausted, pounded Ali had found the strength for this punch, a straight right to Foreman's jaw. Foreman took the punch, recoiled for a second, then slowly crumpled to the canvas.

Pandemonium. The crowd screamed "Ali, Bomaye!" as the referee counted Foreman out. "Muhammad Ali has done it!" broadcaster David Frost yelled into his microphone. "The great man has done it! This is the most joyous scene ever seen in the history of boxing! This is an incredible scene! The place is going wild! Muhammad Ali has won!"[10]

Shortly after regaining the world heavyweight championship, Ali received an invitation from President Gerald Ford to visit the White House. It had been a decade since Cassius X had first antagonized Middle America with his conversion to Islam, and seven years since Muhammad Ali had been stripped of his title for refusing to compromise those religious beliefs. After all that time, all that work, all that pain, Ali had finally redeemed himself. To be welcomed at the White House by a conservative Republican president confirmed what everyone knew to be true: He was a national hero.

"You better watch it," joked Ali as he shook hands with Ford. "I'm out to get your job."[11]

10

The Greatest

"When I'm champ," proclaimed eighteen-year-old Cassius Clay in 1960, "I'll fight anybody who comes along—long as the price is right. The champion owes it to his public. He should be able to whip anybody in the world."[1]

As champion, Muhammad Ali was as good as his word. On October 1, 1975, he gave Joe Frazier another shot at the title. Once again, he chose a developing Third World nation to host the fight. Ali-Frazier III took place in the steaming Filipinos Coliseum in Manila.

Only 25,000 fans could fit into the stadium, but millions more watched on closed-circuit television. If Ali-Frazier I wasn't the greatest fight ever, then "The Thrilla in Manila" probably deserves that honor. The fight was scheduled for fifteen rounds, but it turned out to be the only Ali-Frazier fight that didn't go the distance.

Ali dominated early, landing a fusillade of sharp, clean blows. But Frazier took them all and in the sixth round landed a terrific left hook. It was a harder punch than the one with which he floored Ali in The Fight, according to a sportswriter who had ringside seats for both. The well-conditioned Ali took this punch, however, and kept fighting.

As the boxers moved into the middle rounds, Ali began to tire, while Frazier seemed to gather strength. Frazier's legs were holding up well, but Ali's blows were taking their toll. Yet again, Frazier's face began to swell grotesquely. Soon he had trouble seeing out of his left eye.

"The Thrilla in Manila"

In the twelfth round, Ali regained command of the fight, landing so many combinations that Frazier simply had to slow down. In the thirteenth, Ali hit Frazier with a vicious left hook that knocked the challenger's mouthpiece into the crowd. When Frazier came out for the fourteenth, his left eye was completely closed. Ali now began to take his time, confident that the staggered Frazier could no longer counterattack.

When the bell rang to end the fourteenth round, Frazier walked back to his corner having taken Ali's best, still on his feet. And now it was Ali who looked exhausted. The champ's cornermen looked worried as Ali slumped in his stool. Moments earlier he had been in total control, and now it seemed as though he didn't even have the strength to answer the bell for the last round.

"I thought maybe Ali had punched himself out," Frazier's trainer, Eddie Futch, remembered.[2] Perhaps there was still a chance for victory, Futch thought. But when he looked at his own fighter, he knew the fight was over. Frazier's face was swollen beyond recognition. He could barely pick up his arms. If Ali could in fact answer the bell, it was very likely that he could seriously injure Frazier with a single punch. Futch put his hand on Frazier's shoulder and said, "Joe, it's over. I don't want you to go out there for the next round."[3] Frazier began to protest, but Futch insisted. He threw in the towel, a symbolic gesture indicating that the fight was over. Ali had won. After three fights and forty-one of the most brutal rounds in boxing history, Ali had finally knocked out Joe Frazier.

After Futch's decision to quit was announced, Ali—his face swollen, his legs like lead—stood and threw his arms up in the air. Then his knees buckled, and he collapsed back into his corner. "If God ever calls me to a holy war," Muhammad Ali has said, "I want Joe Frazier fighting beside me."[4]

Even though he won The Thrilla in Manila, it had become obvious that Ali's skills were significantly in decline. The history of sports is filled with athletes who didn't know when to quit. In boxing, particularly, men have continued to fight past their prime, doing serious damage to their bodies and their minds. Ali seemed to be slipping down this dangerous path. He had briefly declared after beating Foreman that he would retire from the ring. Why didn't he? Why didn't he retire after the third Frazier fight?

Ali had financial responsibilities, of course. In 1977, he divorced his second wife, Belinda, and married a model named Veronica Porche. That gave him a wife, four children, and two ex-wives to support, in addition to a sometimes greedy entourage of hangers-on and wheeler-dealers. But Ali had earned more money than any boxer in history, a gross of over $50 million. Surely, this was enough.

Besides, Ali had other skills to fall back on. In 1976, he published his autobiography, *The Greatest*. And over the next few years, he starred in two movies, one based on *The Greatest* and the other a story of runaway slaves called *Freedom Road*. With his remarkable charisma and the boyish good looks that had somehow survived twenty years in the ring, Ali seemed a natural to make the transition to the silver screen. So why did he continue to box?

"The key is, the kid likes boxing," Angelo Dundee explained. "He likes the sport, running in the morning, hanging around the gym, all the excitement building up to a title fight. And wouldn't you like something if you were the best in the world at it?"[5]

But Ali could not be the best forever. On February 15, 1978, a few weeks after his thirty-sixth birthday, Ali took on a young and inexperienced slugger named Leon Spinks. Although it was obvious even before the fight that Ali was not in top condition, he was nevertheless expected to finish off the untested Spinks early, this being only the challenger's eighth professional fight.

The result shocked the world. Ali was slow and heavy, while Spinks put up the fight of his life. Spinks made it through all fifteen rounds with the champ and won a split decision. Although Ali would train intensely and defeat Spinks later that year, winning the title for a record third time, the first Spinks fight was undeniable proof that—in the ring, at least—Ali was no longer the Greatest. Ali retired after the second Spinks fight.

But the lure of the ring and the excitement of a title bout proved to be too strong for Ali to resist. In November, 1980, he climbed through the ropes for one more title fight against the new champion, Larry Holmes, another former sparring partner. Using all the promotional tricks he had learned over the years, Ali had somehow convinced people that he could, at age 38, complete a seemingly impossible comeback and win the heavyweight title a fourth time.

He never had a chance. Holmes did more than overpower Ali—he embarrassed the man. The image of Ali's defeat was carried in newspapers all over the world: There he was, "the Greatest," slumped on his stool, flabby, head down, beaten.

In the years following the Holmes debacle, Ali rarely appeared in public. There was one more fight, another embarrassment against Trevor Berbick in 1981. Rumors spread that Ali was seriously ill, that boxing had left him brain-damaged. The few times he did appear in public, Ali seemed distracted and vacant, with nothing much to talk about, not even himself. And most disturbing of all, when he did speak, he slurred his words.

In 1984, Ali was diagnosed as having Parkinson's Syndrome, a neurological condition similar to Parkinson's Disease but without that disease's degenerative pattern. Its symptoms were tremors, slurred speech, slowness of movement, and rigidity of muscles. Ali's doctors believed it was brought on by the repeated blows to the head he suffered, particularly during his final two or three fights.

After his examination of Ali in 1984, Parkinson's specialist Dr. Stanley Fahn rated his patient as being able to perform all the activities of daily living at 90 percent of what would have been normal for him without his physical condition. "I'm in no pain," Ali told a reporter in 1988. "A slight slurring of my speech, a little tremor. Nothing critical.... If you told me I could go back in my life and start over healthy and that with boxing this would happen—stay Cassius Clay and it wouldn't—I'd take this route. It was worth it."[6] Nevertheless, in recent years, many groups, including the American Medical Association, have called for a ban on boxing. Ali's own medical condition has frequently been cited as but one example of the harm that boxing can do.

"I don't want anyone to feel sorry for me," Ali told his biographer, Thomas Hauser. "...It would be bad if I had a disease that was contagious. Then I couldn't play with children and hug people all over the world. But my problem with speaking bothers other people more than it bothers me. It doesn't stop me from doing what I want to do and being what I want to be. Sometimes I think that too many people put me on a pedestal before and made me into an idol. And that's against Islam; there are no idols in Islam. So maybe this problem I have is God's way of reminding me and everyone else about what's important. I accept it as God's will. And I know that God never gives anyone a burden that's too heavy for them to carry."[7]

Though no longer commanding headlines as a fighter, Ali did maintain his fame. A poll taken in 1983 found him to be the most famous man in the world. In Africa and the Middle East, where he remained most popular, he used his notoriety among Muslims to launch a series of business ventures. He also undertook a great deal of charitable work in developing countries. In December, 1990, he used his personal influence to encourage Saddam Hussein to release fifteen American hostages from Iraq prior to the Persian Gulf War.

In middle age, Ali also seemed to have established a happy and stable personal life. In the summer of 1986, Ali and his third wife divorced, and Ali married for a fourth time. His new bride was Yolanda Williams, known as "Lonnie," also from Louisville, where Lonnie's mother had been good friends with Odessa Clay. Lonnie Ali's degree in business administration enabled her to help her husband sort out his business affairs.

By the late 1980s, Ali was devoting most of his time to his activities as a lay minister for the American Muslim Mission. The church—led by another of Elijah Muhammad's sons, Imam Warithuddin Muhammad—espoused racial tolerance. The Nation of Islam, which remained separatist, had been taken over by the Reverend Louis Farrakhan, with whom Ali had no association whatsoever. Ali had often said that his main concern was to correct what he believed to be the public misconception of the Islamic religion.

"Since [I was young], my beliefs have changed," Ali has said. "I don't believe in Mr. Yacub and the spaceship anymore. ...But Elijah Muhammad was a good man, even if he wasn't the Messenger of God we thought he was. If you look at what our people were like then, a lot of us didn't have self-respect. ...[Elijah Muhammad] made people dress properly, so they weren't on the streets looking like prostitutes and pimps. He taught good eating habits, and was against alcohol and drugs. I think he was wrong when he talked about white devils, but part of what he did was make people feel it was good to be black."[8]

Ali rarely discussed boxing anymore. His days as a fighter were fully behind him. But the boxing world, and the world of sports in general, was forever recast by his presence. When young Cassius Clay turned professional after winning a gold medal in the 1960 Olympics, boxing was a sport dominated by smoky arenas and crooked promoters. Fighters were used and then discarded, living high for a time and then often ending up penniless. By the time Ali retired, however, a title fight meant a multimillion-dollar purse, and it was Muhammad

Ali who made those purses possible. His personal charisma broke through the usual cardboard stereotype of the modest star athlete and showed people that Muhammad Ali was his own man, with his own ideas of right and wrong. The personal authority later wielded by a Michael Jordan or a Magic Johnson derived, in large part, from the independence shown by Ali.

During his career, Muhammad Ali continually stepped outside the mold of what was expected of him. He refused to accept the limitations society placed on him and fought diligently to be accepted on his own terms. He chose banishment from his profession and the scorn of the public rather than compromise his religious beliefs. His triumphant return to the ring proved that, eventually, he got the respect he deserved.

"I always felt like I was born to do something for my people. Eight years old, ten years old; I'd walk out of my house at two in the morning, and look up at the sky for a revelation or God telling me what to do.... God made us all, but some of us are made special. Einstein wasn't an ordinary human. Columbus wasn't an ordinary human. Elvis Presley, the Wright brothers. Some people have special resources inside. And when God blesses you to have more than others, you have a responsibility to use it right."[9]

Important Events in Muhammad Ali's Life

1942   Born January 17 in Louisville, Kentucky.

1954   Fights first televised bout on "Tomorrow's Champions."

1960   Wins a gold medal at the Olympic Games in Rome.

        Makes professional debut against Tunney Hunsaker.

1964   Wins heavyweight title, defeating Sonny Liston.

        Announces his conversion to the Nation of Islam.

1967   Refuses induction into the United States Army and is subsequently stripped of his title and banned from boxing.

1970   Has license renewed and fights for the first time since his banishment, defeating Jerry Quarry.

1971   Loses "The Fight" against Joe Frazier in New York's Madison Square Garden.

1974   Beats Frazier in a rematch.

        Wins the heavyweight championship from George Foreman in "The Rumble in the Jungle" in Kinshasa, Zaire.

1975   Beats Frazier again in "The Thrilla in Manila."

1978   Loses the heavyweight title to Leon Spinks and then wins it for a record third time in a rematch.

1980   Loses the heavyweight title to Larry Holmes.

1984   Is diagnosed as suffering from Parkinson's Syndrome.

1986   Marries fourth wife, Yolanda Williams.

1990   Encourages Iraq to free fifteen Americans hostages prior to the Persian Gulf War.

Notes

Chapter 1

1. *New York Times*, April 29, 1967.
2. Muhammad Ali and Richard Durham, *The Greatest* (New York: Random House, 1975), p.165.
3. Ali and Durham, p. 169.
4. *New York Times*, April 29, 1967.

Chapter 2

1. Ali and Durham, p. 45.
2. Dick Schaap, "The Happiest Heavyweight," *Saturday Evening Post*, March 25, 1961.
3. Ali and Durham, p. 37.
4. Schaap, *Saturday Evening Post*, March 25, 1961.
5. *The National*, May 16, 1991.
6. David Rubel, *Fannie Lou Hamer: From Sharecropping to Politics* (Englewood Cliffs, N.J.: Silver Burdett, 1990), p. 35.
7. Robert M. Lipsyte, *Free to be Muhammad Ali* (New York: Harper & Row, 1978), p. 13.
8. Ali and Durham, pp. 39-40.
9. Robert Lipsyte, "Cassius Clay," *New York Times Magazine*, October 25, 1964.
10. Angelo Dundee, "Hot Corner," *Sports Illustrated*, August 14, 1967.
11. Lipsyte, *Free to be Muhammad Ali*, p. 18.
12. Lipsyte, *Free to be Muhammad Ali*, pp. 13-14.
13. Ali and Durham, p. 51.
14. Schaap, *Saturday Evening Post*, March 25, 1961.
15. Dundee, *Sports Illustrated*, August 14, 1967.
16. Ali and Durham, pp. 67-68.

Chapter 3

1. John Kieran and Arthur Daley, *The Story of the Olympic Games 776 B.C. to 1968* (Philadelphia: J.B. Lippincott, 1969), p. 321.
2. Schaap, *Saturday Evening Post*, March 25, 1961.
3. Schaap, *Saturday Evening Post*, March 25, 1961.
4. Schaap, *Saturday Evening Post*, March 25, 1961.
5. Harry Carpenter, *Boxing: A Pictorial History* (Chicago: Henry Regenery, 1975), p.167.
6. Schaap, *Saturday Evening Post*, March 25, 1961.
7. Schaap, *Saturday Evening Post*, March 25, 1961.
8. *Newsweek*, September 16, 1960.
9. Lipsyte, *Free to be Muhammad Ali*, pp. 3-4.
10. Ali and Durham, p. 66.

Chapter 4

1. Dundee, *Sports Illustrated*, August 14, 1967.
2. Angelo Dundee, "He Could Go to Jail and Still Be Champ," *Sports Illustrated*, August 21, 1967.
3. Lipsyte, *Free to be Muhammad Ali*, p. 33.
4. Lipsyte, *Free to be Muhammad Ali*, p. 34.
5. A.J. Liebling, "The Sporting Scene," *The New Yorker*, March 30, 1963.
6. Carpenter, p. 48.
7. Chris Mead, *Champion: Joe Louis* (New York: Scribner's, 1985), p. 63.
8. Teresa Celsi, *Jesse Jackson and Political Power* (Brookfield, Ct.: Millbrook, 1991), p. 8.

Chapter 5

1. Ali and Durham, p. 106.
2. *The National*, May 15, 1991.
3. *The National*, May 15, 1991.
4. *The National*, May 15, 1991.
5. *The National*, May 15, 1991.
6. *The National*, May 15, 1991.
7. Ali and Durham, p. 111.
8. *The National*, May 15, 1991.
9. *The National*, May 15, 1991.
10. Ali and Durham, p. 111.
11. Ali and Durham, p. 111.
12. Ali and Durham, p. 114.

13. Ali and Durham, p. 115.
14. Ali and Durham, p. 104.
15. Malcolm X with Alex Haley, *The Autobiography of Malcolm X* (New York: Grove Press, 1978), p. 301.
16. George Plimpton, "Miami Notebook: Cassius Clay and Malcolm X," *Harper's*, June, 1964.
17. *The National*, May 16, 1991.
18. Ali and Durham, p. 107.

Chapter 6
1. Thomas Hauser, *Muhammad Ali* (New York: Simon & Schuster, 1991), p. 61.
2. *The National*, May 15, 1991.
3. *The National*, May 15, 1991.
4. *The National*, May 15, 1991.
5. Dundee, *Sports Illustrated*, August 21, 1967.
6. *The National*, May 15, 1991.
7. Ali and Durham, p. 111.
8. Lipsyte, *Free to be Muhammad Ali*, p. 45.
9. Lipsyte, *Free to be Muhammad Ali*, p. 47.
10. Lipsyte, *New York Times Magazine*, October 25, 1964.
11. Hauser, p. 63.
12. Lipsyte, *Free to be Muhammad Ali*, p. 66.
13. "Boxing's Feet of Clay," *Saturday Evening Post*, November 14, 1964.
14. Carpenter, p. 132.
15. Howard Cosell, *Cosell* (Chicago: Playboy Press, 1973), p. 181.
16. Lipsyte, *Free to be Muhammad Ali*, pp. 59-60.
17. *Sports Illustrated*, October 11, 1965.
18. Robert Lipsyte, "I'm Free To Be Who I Want," *New York Times Magazine*, May 28, 1967.

Chapter 7
1. Ali and Durham, p. 129.
2. Lipsyte, *New York Times Magazine*, May 28, 1967.
3. Lipsyte, *New York Times Magazine*, May 28, 1967.
4. Lipsyte, *New York Times Magazine*, May 28, 1967.

5. Ali and Durham, p. 143.
6. Dundee, *Sports Illustrated*, August 21, 1967.
7. Lipsyte, *New York Times Magazine*, May 28, 1967.
8. Angelo Dundee, "Ali and Dundee," *Sports Illustrated*, August 28, 1967.

Chapter 8
1. Lipsyte, *Free to be Muhammad Ali*, p. 87.
2. Cosell, p. 211.
3. Norman Mailer, *Existential Errands* (Boston: Little Brown, 1972), p, 21.
4. Mailer, *Existential Errands*, p. 22.
5. Lipsyte, *Free to be Muhammad Ali*, p. 96.
6. Lipsyte, *Free to be Muhammad Ali*, p. 97.

Chapter 9
1. Cosell, p. 219.
2. Ali and Durham, p. 29.
3. *The National*, May 17-19, 1991.
4. Norman Mailer, *The Fight* (Boston: Little Brown, 1975), p. 15.
5. Mailer, *The Fight*, p. 56
6. Ali and Durham, p. 394.
7. Lipsyte, *Free to be Muhammad Ali*, p. 103.
8. Mailer, *The Fight*, p. 179.
9. Mailer, *The Fight*, p. 180.
10. Mailer, *The Fight*, p. 208.
11. Lipsyte, *Free to be Muhammad Ali*, p. 106.

Chapter 10
1. Schaap, *Saturday Evening Post*, March 25, 1961.
2. *The National*, May 17-19, 1991.
3. *The National*, May 17-19, 1991.
4. *The National*, May 17-19, 1991.
5. Lipsyte, *Free to be Muhammad Ali*, p. 114.
6. Thomas Hauser, "Still The Greatest," *New York Times Magazine*, July 17, 1988.
7. *The National*, May 21, 1991.
8. Hauser, p. 97.
9. Hauser, p. 18.

Suggested Reading

MUHAMMAD ALI

Edwards, Audrey, and Gary Wohl. *Muhammad Ali: The People's Champ*. New York: Little, Brown, 1977.

Hauser, Thomas. *Muhammad Ali*. New York: Simon & Schuster, 1991.

Ruden, Kenneth. *Muhammad Ali*. New York: Harper Junior Books, 1976.

Rummel, Jack. *Muhammad Ali*. New York: Chelsea House, 1989.

BOXING

Boxer Champions, 1952-1987. Camino, Cal.: Camino, 1988.

Morrison, Ian. *Boxing: The Records*. Middlesex, England: Guinness Publishing, 1988.

Rainbolt, Richard. *Boxing's Heavyweight Champions*. Minneapolis, Minn.: Lerner Publishing, 1975.

Schroeder, Charles R. *Boxing Skills for Fun and Fitness*. Memphis, Tenn.: Regmar Publications, 1973.

Thomas, Art, and Laura Storms. *Boxing is for Me*. Minneapolis, Minn.: Lerner Publishing, 1982.

Index

Agent Orange, 68
Ali, Belinda Boyd (second wife),
    71, 89
Ali, Jamillah (daughter), 71
Ali, Maryum (daughter), 71
Ali, Muhammad
    acts in Broadway show, 71
    adopts name of Cassius X,
        51
    adopts name of Muham-
        mad Ali, 57
    amateur bouts, 25-26
    convicted of draft evasion,
        71
    divorces Belinda, 89
    draft notice, 65-66, 69-70
    Angelo Dundee becomes
        trainer, 37-39
    fight with Ernie Terrell
        cancelled, 65-68
    fights George Foreman,
        82-86
    fights Joe Frazier, 74-79, 82,
        87-89
    fights Larry Holmes, 91
    fights Sonny Liston, 47, 51,
        53-56, 60-63
    fights Ken Norton, 81, 82
    fights Floyd Patterson,
        63-64, 80
    fights Jerry Quarry, 74, 80
    fights Leon Spinks, 90
    first fight, 23
    first visit to boxing gym,
        17
    goes to work for Billy
        Reynolds, 26-27
    indicted for draft evasion,
        14
    invited to White House, 86
    marries Belinda Boyd, 71
    marries Veronica Porche,
        89
    marries Sonji Roi, 58

    marries Yolanda Williams,
        92-93
    Archie Moore becomes
        trainer, 37
    and Nation of Islam, 47-51
    and Parkinson's Syndrome,
        91-92
    refuses induction into
        army, 13-14, 69-70
    relations with press, 40-41
    speaks at college campus-
        es, 71
    takes up boxing, 22-23
    wins Amateur Athletic
        Union title, 26
    wins Golden Gloves title,
        25-26
    wins Olympic gold medal,
        15, 26, 29-31
Ali, Muhammad, Jr. (son), 71
Ali, Rasheda (daughter), 71
Ali, Sonji Roi (first wife), 57-58
Ali, Veronica Porche (third wife),
    89
Ali, Yolanda Williams (fourth
    wife), 92-93
American Medical Association,
    92
American Muslim Mission, 93
Assassination
    of Robert Kennedy, 73
    of Martin Luther King, Jr.,
        73
    of Malcolm X, 61

Becus, Yvon, 30
Berbick, Trevor, 91
Blackburn, Jack, 41-42
Black Muslims, 48-51, 56-57, 58
Blair, Ezell, Jr., 33
Bonavena, Oscar, 74
Brown, Drew (Bundini), 51, 85
Brown v. Board of Education, 33
Buck White, 71

Carnera, Primo, 44
Chicago Tribune, 84
Churchill Downs, 18
Clay, Cassius Marcellus (Cash), Sr.
    (father), 18, 19, 20, 36
Clay, Cassius Marcellus, Jr. *See*
    Ali, Muhammad.
Clay, Herman (grandfather), 20
Clay, Odessa (mother), 19
Closed-circuit television, 43
Conrad, Harold, 45, 46
Cooper, Henry, 46-47
Covington, Hayden, 11

D'Amato, Cus, 36
Davis, Jefferson, 18
Dundee, Angelo, 24, 26, 37, 54,
    55, 68, 70, 84, 90
Dunkley, Lt. S. Steven, 12-13

Eisenhower, Dwight, 33
Ellis, Jimmy, 71-72, 80
Eskridge, Chauncey, 11

Fahn, Dr. Stanley, 91
Farrakhan, Louis, 93
"The Fight," 75-79
Ford, Gerald, 86
Foreman, George, 80-81, 82-86
Foster, Bob, 80
Frazier, Joe, 72, 74-79, 80-81, 82,
    87-89
Freedom Road, 90
Frost, David, 86
Futch, Eddie, 89

Golden Gloves championship,
    25-26
Gorgeous George, 39
The Greatest, 90

Hartman, Lt. Clarence, 13
Hauser, Thomas, 92
Ho Chi Minh, 66-67
Hodges, Quinton, 11
Holmes, Larry, 84, 91
Hoover, Herbert, 32
Humphrey, Hubert, 72, 73
Hunsaker, Tunney, 36

Hussein, Saddam, 92

Illinois Athletic Commission,
    67-68
International Boxing Club (IBC),
    42-43

Jackson, Jesse, 42
Jeffries, Jim, 41
Johnson, Jack, 22, 41
Johnson, Lyndon, 60, 72
Johnson, Rafer, 30
Justice Department, 70

Kennedy, Robert, 72, 73
King, Martin Luther, Jr., 32-33, 73

Liebling, A.J., 41
Lincoln, Abraham, 18
Lipsyte, Robert, 69-70
Liston, Sonny, 44-47, 51, 53-56,
    60-63
Little, Malcolm. *See* Malcolm X.
London, Jack, 41
Louis, Joe, 23, 36, 41-42
Louisville Sponsoring Group, 37,
    38, 68
Lunch counter sit-ins, 33-34

MacDonald, Bill, 51
Maddox, Lester, 74
Madigan, Tony, 30
Madison Square Garden, 76, 82
Mailer, Norman, 75
Malcolm X, 48-51, 61
Marciano, Rocky, 42
Marshall, Marty, 45
Martin, Joe, 17, 23, 25
McCain, Franklin, 33
McCarthy, Eugene, 72
McKee, Lt. Col. J. Edwin, 13
McNeil, Joseph, 33
Mobutu Sese Seko, 83
Montgomery Bus Boycott, 32-33
Moore, Archie, 37, 40
Muhammad, Elijah, 47-48, 57,
    61, 93
Muhammad, Herbert, 57, 68
Muhammad, Imam, 93

Nasser, Gamal Abdel, 58
Nation of Islam, 47-51, 56-60,
  61, 93
Nazareth College, 25
New York Times, 57
Nilon, Jack, 47
Nixon, Richard, 73
Nkrumah, Kwame, 58
North Carolina Agricultural and
  Technical College, 33
Norton, Ken, 81, 82

O'Keefe, Ronnie, 23
Olympic Games, 29-31
Organization for Afro-American
  Unity, 61

Parkinson's Syndrome, 91-92
Parks, Rosa, 32
Pastrano, Willie, 24, 26
Patterson, Floyd, 30, 43, 44, 45,
  46, 63-64, 80
Persian Gulf War, 92
Pietrzykowski, Zbigniew, 30-31
Poole, Elijah. *See* Muhammad,
  Elijah.
Presley, Elvis, 37, 80
Press, Ali's relations with, 40-41
Press conferences, 56-57, 66

Quarry, Jerry, 74, 80

Rademacher, Pete, 36
Reynolds, Billy, 26-27, 31-32, 36
Richmond, David, 33
Robbins, Dr. Alexander, 54
Robinson, Jackie, 41
Robinson, Sugar Ray, 23-24, 36
Roman, Joe, 82
Rudolph, Wilma, 30
"The Rumble in the Jungle,"
  82-86

Sabedong, Duke, 39
Saturday Evening Post, 58
Schmeling, Max, 23, 42
Segregation, 19
Selective Service System, 65
Shatkov, Gennady, 30

Sit-ins, 33-34
Spinks, Leon, 90
State Department, 70
Supreme Court, 71, 80

Television, closed-circuit, 43
Terrell, Ernie (The Octopus),
  65-68
Tet Offensive, 72
"The Thrilla in Manila," 87-89
Thunderbird Hotel, Las Vegas, 44
Till, Emmett, 21-22
"Tomorrow's Champions," 23
Tunney, Gene, 67
Tyson, Mike, 45

*United States of America v. Cassius
  Marsellus Clay*, 70, 80

Vietnam War, 60-61, 66-67, 72

Waldorf Astoria Hotel, New
  York, 32
Westmoreland, William C., 11, 72
Willard, Jess, 41
Wilson, Atwood, 26

Thomas Conklin has won awards for his work as a writer and editor of children's magazines. He is also a playwright, and is currently working for the Williamstown Theater Festival. He lives in Maplewood, New Jersey.